Freeman's
Power

Previous Issues

Freeman's
Power

Est. 2015

Edited by

John Freeman

Grove Press UK

THE NEW SCHOOL
CREATIVE WRITING

Contents

CONTENTS

Introduction

JOHN FREEMAN

When I was a child, I had an obsession with speedometers. I rode around on my bike peering in one driver-side window after another, noting the top speed of all the neighbors' cars. This was the late 1970s during the gasoline crisis, so a lot of dials topped out at 75 or 85 mph. Even the font used for these numbers seemed apologetic, and serious, like it was actually saying, *You really shouldn't be going this fast*. Older and foreign cars provided more thrills. I still feel the shock of looking into a 1955 Chevy and seeing "120" on the gauge. I tooled home for dinner, that miraculous number turning in my head.

Back then my own top speed was around 14 mph, so these numbers were more than trivia. They were a kind of imagined agency. Every single thing I loved back then had some form of locomotive agency. It pierced the earth's atmosphere or burned a stripe of rubber at the drag strip or unzippered a lake's calm. I moved significantly only when an adult decided I should. I didn't envy the drivers of fast and powerful things, I envied the vehicles themselves. My dream was to be a truck driver. How wonderful it would be, I thought, to have a strapping friend to explore the world in, sleep in at night, talk to as miles peeled by.

Eventually, I got my chance. In 1984, my family moved to California. A trucking van not much smaller than our house parked outside and men shoved all our worldly belongings into its mouth. We set off in our tiny brown station wagon across the country, and "Kool"—as the stenciled door of his big rig announced him—followed behind. The plan was to stop every 800 miles or so with a friend or family member, see the country. My father was forty-five years old that year, older than I am as I type this. I try to imagine what it would be like to start my life over with three children and nothing but the anchor of a new job that could go badly, and I marvel.

We arrived in Sacramento a day before Kool, who parked his truck beneath our enormous new palm tree. I climbed into his cab as my grandfather, uncle, and father talked. I was bewildered by the big rig's gauges, amazed by the height of its ride, and confused by how the truck seemed to be floating, almost going backward. In fact, it was: I'd depressed an air brake, and four tons of moving van had begun rolling toward the men unloading it. Kool hopped up into the truck in a single bound, and shoved me aside. *Look out man,* he shouted, *you're going to kill someone.* My uncle, who had always spoken to me as if I were an equal, took me aside afterward, knelt down, and said the same. *This could have been a terrible day.*

Those words haunted me upon our arrival in California. Partly because I knew, in some obscure fashion, that I was drawn into that truck by a feeling of powerlessness. I'd spent three weeks trapped in our family car, carted across the country, not much freer than the family dog, watching as people freer than me went about their adventures. I wanted power like theirs. I was tired of imagining it; the time had come for me to have some for myself. I didn't think I was actually going to drive away in Kool's rig, but I wanted to know what it'd feel like. Sort of like holding an unloaded gun.

In light of the possible consequences, this desire seemed suddenly to me like a form of greed. It made me ashamed, and it would later dawn on me that all around forked other forms of power. The power of my imagination, to envision the horror scene Kool had very barely averted; the power of my father's forgiveness, which washed over me days later like the cool of a cloud stepping in front of the sun; the power of the sun itself, bolting down on us in Sacramento, even in the fall, erasing in all its yellow light the past just like that; and the power of love, which I felt from my grandmother whom we'd left behind. I could see her sitting at her writing desk, the lake we used to visit behind her. To feel her warmth from such a distance merely from her letters? That was a power. Everything that was, I discovered, was enacted by power. Having power meant nothing—it was valuable depending on *how* you deployed it.

It says something that in our current political context, an issue of *Freeman's* themed to power may come trailed by an expectation that this will be an issue about the flagrant and breathtaking abuses of power ongoing right now across the globe. I thought of doing this. We are indeed living in a time of power grabbing, of economic sadism, which is to say violence. And there has been precious little leadership from people who possess the greatest power. At the time of this writing, the president of the United States is not unlike a little boy who has climbed up into a huge truck he's always wanted to possess. And already he has run over people. He doesn't even care.

One of the degradations of the recent period, though, is how abuses of power can reduce our definition of power itself. The abiding fantasy of so many, after all, myself included, is to expose corrupt leaders and this current president. To bring them lower than they've brought people they abused. This is a fantasy like jumping into the truck, though. There are so many other vectors of power slicing through life, from the power of generosity to the power of taking over one's story, and it is this enlarged sense of what power is—not just the power to take, or to dominate—wherein lies our salvation.

In this sense, the issue of *Freeman's* you hold in your hand is an attempt to look at how power operates in the world. And I hope it simultaneously recalibrates the balance of power through that observation. *I see you,* many of these pieces say; *I see you seeing me, and here's what you're missing.* In her ferocious essay, Aminatta Forna describes all the ways being a woman of color on the street requires constant vigilance regarding how power is being used to frame her. She speaks back. She looks back. She's tired of having to assess when those actions are dangerous.

Violence lurks within the frame of every single one of these pieces. Growing up in Israel, Etgar Keret learns that the willingness to inflict harm is a great form of power—something the hero of Eka Kurni-awan's story grapples with, too. In her startling essay on suicide, Nicole Im turns to the behavior of sharks to meditate on how a willingness to stop pain by turning it on oneself does not necessar-ily mean freedom. In her poem, "Update on Werewolves," Margaret Atwood sees a need to update the horror genre for a world in which women have more power than before, and that danger exists when any power runs amok.

Power that is projected does not always see itself as power—this is one of the many necessary adjustments Me Too has been making, pointing out such entitlements. For too long, at the receiving end of power, women have become doctorates of power negotiations, and several pieces here describe how this happens in the domestic setting. In Lan Samantha Chang's short story, a Chinese immigrant's resentment over her husband's power to say no leads her to take a staggering financial gamble. Meantime, across the world in Bangla-desh, Tahmima Anam imagines a woman resurrecting her family's well-being by selling bull semen. In her short essay, Eula Biss con-templates the way burlesquing domination and subjugation does not always happen in performances: it can accidentally happen at home.

Telling stories about power can too easily be seen as a form of *empowerment*, a word many writers here distrust. In her essay on working as a life drawing model, Josephine Rowe describes how standing nude before a group of painters taught her the value of interior life, not of any kind of love of her body. Writing on the so-called Stockholm syndrome, Nimmi Gowrinathan notes how discomfiting anger can be. Édouard Louis's father spent a life working in factories, and in telling that story Louis finds himself becoming an investigator of an economic homicide. He wants to find out who is to blame. In retrospect, watching Grenfell Tower burn, Ben Okri has a sense of why mass murder has happened there: "In this age of austerity/The poor die for others' prosperity," he writes.

It requires love to see the wreck we've made of the world and not wrap ourselves in despair. This means breaking down the conception of sight as knowledge, when it in fact is so often just another form of power. Leïla Slimani speaks to Moroccan women whose sexuality is shrouded in secrecy and finds that out of this burden of silence they form stronger bonds with each other for protection. After all, most of them live at the whims of men. In their reportage from Syria, Chris Russell and Patrick Hilsman talk to a young man who explains the way the Assad regime used the dispersal of truth on the Internet to crack down on resistance. No one knew what to believe. All of this has led many people closer and closer to their own families.

Modern technology, as seen through many of these pieces, does little to create a public space of equality—let alone redistribute power fairly. In a short riff about a peasant being filmed in China, A Yi notes the man's confusion and fear as he suddenly has to decide how to perform himself for a group that isn't even there. That's the power of the media. A related form of doubling comes to haunt the narrator of David Mitchell's story, who starts to notice that a man is following him across key moments of his life.

The ultimate maze is language itself, and several writers here turn their gaze on what it teaches them as they learn to use it. Aleksandar Hemon reveals how so much history lurks in the words Bosnians use, where they come from, and what they occlude. Growing up in the garlic fields of Central California, decades later, Jaime Cortez learns something similar when he and his siblings stumble on a collection of pornography. Riding across a post-9/11 New York of bomb threats and amber alerts, Deborah Landau unpeels the way language of terror velvets its participants in irrational, sexualized fear. The heroine of Kanako Nishi's story feels how language slides so easily into control: watching a man burn items from his home behind her house, she asks him keenly, "Can you burn words?"

Of course you can't, but you can shine a light on ways power has always emerged from places one assumes to be powerless. Julia Alvarez writes of how she grew up reading books without the heroines she wanted—and part of her life was created by that longing. Elif Shafak fondly remembers time with her grandmother, and muses on how she was raised by a woman with an old form of knowledge and power, while her mother attended a university and acquired for herself a more modern way of accessing power. In her beautiful poem Jenni Fagan creates an odyssey of sorts for people who never left home, revealing that to name a person—a friend—is a powerful act of self-preservation.

We are born into this world nameless and feral, and our lives can be seen as a long attempt to undo these conditions. In her prose poem, the US poet laureate Tracy K. Smith uncovers a loss in this domestication, an impeding subtraction that makes children at a certain age all the more feral. Once they have been civilized out of us these early instincts are hard to restore. Certain leaders in the political sphere often appeal, in essence, to the feeling that what we gave up mattered.

Traveling the world in the last five decades, Barry Lopez has made it his calling never to forget our animal nature. But rather than interpret it as brute force, time and again he remembers how—when stripped of our collective power, or a gun—humans are very small things. In his luminescent essay, "Fourteen Aspects of Power," Lopez gently reminds us that power is juxtapositional, and there is a moral responsibility in that comparison. In his eyes, we must keep tilting the world to see it anew—that is in essence the best of what humans can be. Students of comparison. Not always jumping into the truck, but thinking about who is behind it.

Six Shorts

KNOWING

One of my earliest memories is of Grandma melting pieces of lead in a tiny pot and then pouring the ash-grey liquid into a bowl of salted water. A sizzling sound. A strong smell. I held my breath, waiting without knowing for what, overwhelmed by both excitement and fear.

Each time she did this the melted lead would assume a different shape. Grandma would study its form in silence, her face pure concentration.

"Grandma . . ."

"Hmmm?"

"What do you see in there?" I asked. "Tell me, what's happening?"

"Shush. You're scaring it."

I was scaring what exactly? The water? The molten metal? Someone's destiny? Or an invisible djinni hopping and dancing around us in the room? Grandma did not care to answer. Then, a bit later, seeing my puzzled face, she called me.

I sat on her lap, inhaling the scent of rose water, crushed cinnamon and toasted sesame that emanated from her clothes. Cautiously, I squinted into the bowl, just as I had seen her do a hundred times. I tried to get a good view of the mysteries bubbling and swirling in there. I saw nothing.

I had started school that same autumn, and although I already knew how to read, it soon became obvious that writing would be a massive challenge. There was a problem: I was left-handed. Our teacher had told me—in front of all the other children—that if I wanted to get a red velvet ribbon like everyone else, I'd better send my left hand into exile. I had never heard that word before, "exile." Where was this place? How could I go there? And, more important, how was I to send a part of me into exile while keeping the remaining part here? Little did I know that it was possible to be torn, to be fragmented, to be divided like that, and to become an insider-outsider, to feel like a stranger in your own motherland.

At the time all of that was unknown to me. Sending my left hand into exile meant keeping it under the desk all day long, and relying on my right hand for everything—writing, holding a book, putting my hand up. The left hand was reserved for dirty things, the teacher had explained. Since time immemorial, the left hand was for sinners and for sinning.

As a result, I started using my right hand and I ended up hating my own handwriting—a feeling that still continues. I did not want to hold a pencil and whenever I had to do so, I would squeeze it so hard between my fingers that it would break into two. What a strange feeling it was having so many things to say but being unable to put them into writing.

So now, as I pointed at the bowl, I made sure to do so with my right hand. "Grandma, what do those holes mean?"

"Those"—she paused, her sea-green eyes lighting up—"Those holes mean if you don't eat your vegetables, and keep rejecting my stewed okra, there's no way you can grow up!"

We were very close, my Grandma and I.

I was born in Strasbourg, France, though both my parents are Turkish. My father, a dedicated academic, was completing his PhD at a French university. My mother, however, had dropped out of university and followed him, thinking love would be enough. But the marriage would not last long and a few years later my mother and I would take a one-way train to Turkey.

One morning we arrived at Grandma's house in Ankara. Only later would I come to understand this was a very conservative, patriarchal, middle-class Muslim neighbourhood.

Having made the terrible mistake of getting married at the tender age of nineteen, my mother had now become a young divorcée. She had no diploma, no money, no career. Immediately our prying neighbours began looking around for a suitable husband for her. But my Grandma intervened. "I believe my daughter should go back to university," she said. "She should have a diploma, a career. She should have choices."

When the same neighbours reminded Grandma that my mother had a toddler to take care of and could therefore not become a student, Grandma said with a shrug, "I'll raise my grandchild. Meanwhile my daughter is free to do as she pleases. She's young. She can build her life anew."

Thus, my mother went back to university to finish her degree and then to build a career.

As for me, I was raised by Grandma, whom I sometimes called "Annemim" (my Mama-ma). And my own mother I usually called "Abla" (big sister). The logic behind this labelling was a bit confusing to everyone else, but somehow crystal clear to me.

Every morning after breakfast Grandma would prepare a cup of bitter coffee for herself and a glass of honeyed milk for me. When she finished her drink, she would turn the cup upside down, wait until it cooled and then peer inside. She didn't watch the news, she didn't read the newspapers; she read coffee grounds instead.

Around midday neighbours and strangers would knock on our door, asking for help. They would all be served tea, a constant tinkling of silver spoons against glass echoing in the house. People with skin diseases, mood disorders, chronic fatigue or depression were among Grandma's regular visitors.

For she was a healer, my Grandma. There were things she could do, and things she couldn't. She was a healer specialized in certain fields.

Should anyone try to make a payment or offer a gift, she would refuse it firmly. When I asked her about this, she said you were given knowledge so that you could pass it on to others. How could you demand money for something you did not own in the first place? Nobody owned knowledge.

It was the late 1970s. Inside the house there were rose thorns, crushed dried chickpeas, evil eye beads, amber rosaries . . . Outside the house there were strikes, gunshots, suicide bombs and demonstrations . . . People died. People disappeared. Far-right were fighting far-left, Kurdish nationalists were fighting Turkish nationalists, even supporters of the same ideology were fighting among themselves.

I remember sitting by the window, looking outside at the turbulent world where my mother was studying, working, struggling to find her way and her freedom. I would worry endlessly about the bombs and the conflicts and the violence. Meanwhile, another part of me would listen to the murmurs in the house, my Grandma's soothing voice.

How could these opposite forces inhabit the same world—my world, that is? The political and the surreal, the public and the deeply personal, my mother's resistance and my grandmother's acceptance . . .

On Sunday mornings, the only days I would see them spend free time together, they would place large, round trays on the table and start making dolma, stuffing spoonfuls of rice and meat and wild herbs inside little green peppers. They didn't talk much, their movements deft and practiced. But their silence was a peaceful one. A harmonious one. A mutual recognition of their different personalities, a sisterhood of sorts. I would prick my ears trying to catch what went unsaid, and open my eyes trying to observe what remained invisible, obsessed with solving the puzzle that they were to me. I was certain they were full of secrets, these two women. What exactly were they hiding from me?

And when the dolmas were ready my Grandma would say, playfully, "Stop watching us as if we were TV. Whatever you see in us is present in you. One day, you'll know. But now, come and eat, sweetheart. Come and eat."

—Elif Shafak

JAMILA
"IN THE INTEREST OF MEN"

I had never in my life talked with my childhood nanny about sex. I would have found it unthinkable to raise the subject with this woman, even though she has been living under our roof for more than twenty years. We represent, the two of us, completely opposite types of women. Fifty years old, she has never married, and if we take seriously the importance she accords to morality and religion, she is a virgin. She lives and works in our home. She supports many members of her family, who turn readily to her whenever there is a problem yet treat her with little consideration: because she is a woman, and because she has no husband. A devout person, she is—I know this—shocked by the way I live. I smoke, I drink, I go out whenever I want. I have as many boys for friends as I do girls. I realize that when I was a teenager, she must have been dumbfounded to see the parties we used to throw, where girls and boys would slow-dance dreamily together.

So I have a rather clear image of my nanny: she's a conservative, and she doubtless judges me without ever saying anything. When my novel came out, I had a chance to form a wholly different picture of her. One evening when we were alone in the kitchen, she remarked, with a naughty look in her eye: "By the way, I know what your book is about." I smiled, a bit flustered by the subject she'd brought up. I was also afraid that she might lecture me. "You're talking about sex maniacs, right?" she continued. "Because you know, in Morocco, there are lots of them. In my neighborhood, many women tell me about this."

First news flash: my so prudish and so moralizing nanny talks about sex with the local women. I'm speechless!

"I have a friend who lives near my old home. She told me that her husband wanted to make love three or four times a day. He doesn't ask what she thinks. You see what I mean?" she adds. Yes, I see, he rapes her. I realize that I don't know how to say "rape" in Arabic, but my nanny and I have understood each other.

"Many men are like that," she goes on. "The women, they work, they raise the children, they keep house. And on top of that, they have to do everything *monsieur* wants and they keep getting pregnant. Fortunately, some men prefer to see other girls in the neighborhood and they leave their wives alone." Other girls? I ask her if she's talking about prostitutes.

"Sure, of course. There are lots of them. Very young ones. You know, even the Saudis come here for the prostitutes. In Rabat, they've had a huge house built for them where they receive really young girls. These girls have to strip stark naked and dance in front of them. After a while, the men throw paper money down and tell them: 'Roll in that, and if you've sweated hard, you can keep all the bills that stick to you.'"

I don't know if this story is entirely true and I have no real way to verify it. Still, it's public knowledge that rich men from the Gulf come regularly to Morocco to take advantage of our unfortunately legendary prostitution. In fact, they find it so palatable that many girls have "exported" themselves to the Gulf region. A migration that isn't to everyone's taste.

"Prostitution means ruin for the women," my nanny continues, clearly determined to tell me everything. "In the neighborhood, you know, there's that girl who has AIDS. She concealed it for a long time, but finally everyone found out. The guy who'd stuck her with it dropped her and disappeared. Now she's completely abandoned. It's sad, everything that happens. In many families, you see girls getting pregnant by their uncle or even their father. The girls don't talk about it. Either they get hidden away, or they kill themselves." I point out to her that all these situations stem from massive hypocrisy and that no one dares to denounce crimes committed under the pretext of warding off dishonor. I try to explain to her that a society in which women had more freedom would not necessarily be contrary to religion, yet would permit better protection for women. To my great surprise, she agrees. "All this," she tells me, "does not serve the cause of Islam. It is solely in the interest of men."

—Leïla Slimani
Translated from the French by Linda Coverdale

HUMBLE HAND

There's a peasant on the TV again. He's thin, with prominent cheekbones, the skin on his face tight and shiny. His eyes are mousy, bright, and darting, always evasive. Evading what? Evading the TV camera.

It was like this the first time he was photographed, and now it's the same the first time he's being filmed. He's come into contact with this high-tech stuff only a few times in his life; it does not fit with his experience, and he only partially understands it. Partial understanding leads to reverence, and the fear that he's somehow doing it wrong. Meanwhile officials of a certain grade are adept at making these machines their handmaidens. Before the bright black glass of the lens they dip and preen; even their clothing exudes a powerful confidence. They take the peasant's hand, no discussion brooked, gripping it powerfully, shaking it powerfully, and then they commence to summon language from their minds. The words come haltingly at first, and they ease themselves through with auxiliary noises like *um* and *ah*. Later, as the words start to surge and flood, they disengage their hands and, like orchestra conductors, begin to conduct the crowd.

At these times, I'm left watching the peasant's hand in horror. He doesn't know whether to allow his fingers to curl naturally, or to keep them extended. It seems foolish to keep his thumb and forefinger spread wide before the camera, but what if he lets his fingers fold up and then the officials double back for another squeeze? Wouldn't that be a breach of etiquette? After due consideration, he decides to leave his hand stuck stiffly in the air—better safe than sorry.

And there it stays, as if paralyzed, dangled absurdly into the torrent of words. Not until the lens turns to follow the departing officials does the hand retract and curl, and tug at his clothes.

As far as the peasant himself is concerned, what matters isn't whether he's one of the neglected elderly, or a victim of the recent hailstorm, or whether nothing's happened at all and he's simply there as backdrop. What matters is that he has survived this moment.

—A Yi
Translated from the Chinese by Eric Abrahamsen

ON RUNNING

I ran, often. I was chased, often, by other boys who wanted to beat me, sometimes by random adults angry at me, mainly for being a child— grown-ups typically hate all children except their own. Sometimes I was chased by strangers. Once, I remember, a postman pursued me, aiming to hurt me, which he did when he caught me, because the world sends out its agents to harm you; they linger out there until such time arrives. There is a pale man in a wool coat and hat across the street looking up this way as we speak, believe me. So I remember myself as a child running toward Kino Arena, along the row of garages; I don't remember who was chasing me. What I do remember was a presence of danger at my heels, and my running as fast as I could, all the while growing aware that I couldn't run any faster. I wanted to accelerate, I willed a greater speed, but the will didn't reach anywhere below my waist, and my legs just couldn't. Whoever was chasing me caught me and beat me; this was how I learned about my limits, about the existence of limits. My will hit the ceiling of my being like a distraught moth. Beyond the ceiling was who knows what, or just plain nothing, solidified into a sky. The details are sketchy and may have come from another moment in my life: at some other time, I must have also been running toward Kino Arena. I ran along that stretch between my building and the movie theater every day of my boyhood—the recollection can't be that specific, so that when I remember the running, my body doesn't respond. But when I remember the chase and my failed attempt to will acceleration, my body responds—it remembers its inability to transcend itself, it swells with sadness; it hurts. It becomes what it's always been: a slow, dying body, ever unable to restore itself, in recollection, or in any other way. It will eventually run out of itself, out of myself. Kino Arena was shelled in the war, and then razed in peacetime. Now, it's a gravel parking lot. When I was a boy, I wanted to be a historian.

ON READING

I once spent three days in a coal shack reading old comic books. I was eight or so; we were visiting my uncle Bogdan in Bijeljina. In World War Two, he fought for freedom with Tito's partisans and received a bullet in his lungs. He had six kids, all of them older than me, my favorite, his daughter Ljilja. His oldest son was already in college; before he left he'd stored away stacks of his old comic books, tied with a rope like ancient manuscripts. They lay in the shack untouched until I discovered and untied them to spend hours on a pile of coal, reading, my parents occasionally ordering me to come out and spend time with living human beings. And I'd come out, pouting, and be with the living human beings until they forgot about me, whereupon I'd sneak back into the coal shack to read more. Fortunately, it rained a bit, so they couldn't force me to come out and play. I don't remember any light in there. I recall reading in complete darkness, as if with X-ray eyes. The eternal life belongs to those who live in the present. The only comic I clearly remember was set in medieval Croatia, at the time of Matija Gubec, the leader of a peasant uprising. The main hero, a young man, fought for freedom in his own special way: he prowled at night scaring the feudal oppressors, dressed in a body suit that made him look like a living skeleton. I didn't know it then, but it's clear to me now that the exhilarating pleasure of reading in the coal shack was related to the darkness that surrounded me. I licked my coal-flavored fingers to turn the pages slowly. Death is not an event in life, but it was reading over my shoulder. I could hear the living call my name.

ON SEARCHING

I'd lock myself in the bathroom and create mixtures of nail polish, aftershave, shampoo, hand cream, and baby powder. I'd light the concoction to see if it'd explode, burn, or at least produce fumes. Or

I'd bunch up newspapers and set them on fire in the tub and pour the hopefully explosive mix onto it. Nothing would happen except that the flakes of incinerated paper would float up to the ceiling to get stuck there like dark clouds. There were no fire alarms in our apartment; we lived happily in a firetrap, armed only with common sense, which I frequently suspended to pursue dangerous knowledge. I sought the perfect mix of ingredients, the exact proportions, assuming that the perfection would become evident in the flames or the explosion; it took me a long while to discover that shampoo doesn't burn, and that hand cream is chemically inert. And it wasn't just bathroom alchemy I was interested in. I also stuck nails into sockets and bare copper wires into electric heaters, daring our apartment, our life, the universe, to either kill me, hurt me, or allow me, at least, to discover what would happen. Nothing ever happened, but I didn't care. You go where the inquiry takes you; you follow the path of knowledge. A new possibility cannot be discovered later. I stuck needles under the skin on my palms, knelt on corn kernels until my knees were bruised and tears ran down my cheeks. I devised recipes for a dish that had never been cooked before, requiring ingredients that could not be found, and I'd prepare it for no one, sometimes starting an oil fire in a pan, and no one would eat it; it was as if I was performing a Black Mass. Later, I searched my parents' closets because I didn't know what their lives were like, who they really were, other than being the people who made me and raised me. I came up with names for things that didn't exist until I discovered they existed. The world is made of strangers, of odd parts and simple objects that strive to be in a space, to be gathered into a whole, like words, like sentences.

ON WORDS

Here we have to enter a linguistic field where we're likely to get lost: while the English word *marble* is a fine one for a glass ball with which children play, the value of *kliker* is far greater to someone like me, whoever he may be. For one thing, the Bosnian word comes from the German *Klicker*, which refers to the sound of the glass balls colliding. I find that beautiful: I hear that sound right now. This suggests that the migration that eventually brought a *kliker* to me started with the Austro-Hungarian occupation force that entered Bosnia in 1878. This is how history works: everything begins far away and long ago, with armies moving, burning cities scalding the sky, children orphaned; everything ends in my body, with my writing about it. But the vocabulary I recall being deployed during the games I played is hard to source, resembling no particular foreign language, having no other application in Bosnian, working only while I was playing with *kliker*s, meaningless otherwise:

roša (the hole in the ground where you wanted to put your *kliker* so as to have the power to eliminate others);

ponte (used when you are demanding from the other players that they throw their *kliker*s toward the *roša*, where yours is sitting, empowered, waiting to eliminate them);

hopa (the last player who throws his *kliker* toward the *roša* at the beginning of each game);

predhopa (the player before the last one to throw);

slipci (dropping two *kliker*s together to resolve a situation in which two *kliker*s find themselves in the *roša*, though this maneuver has to be agreed upon before the game).

There is more, but the list is beginning to look pathetic in its obscure nostalgia. I have reasons to believe that this particular vocabulary made sense only within my neighborhood in Sarajevo, and would've been entirely foreign beyond it. The game is now forgotten, as is the vocabulary, as we all will and must be. I haven't played the game in decades, nor have I seen children playing it, in Sarajevo or anywhere else, at least not since before the war. Here and there, I run into people who can recall and recite the vocabulary, like an ancient poem in a lost language. The word *kliker* is still around, but at present it has no value, because its referent world is obsolete. What we cannot speak about we must pass over in silence. Yet I remember being close to the ground, focused on my *kliker*, lost in a universe of grass and twigs; and I remember the smell and texture of the dirt, its softness perfect for the rolling movement, and the shards of glass like diamonds and pebbles, and the determined earthworms dying in the dry soil, here and there a trail of ants moving toward some horizon apparent only to them. It all used to make sense, which I cannot retrieve now. My friends, some of whom are now dead, followed their own orbits around the *roša*, as if none of them could ever end.

—Aleksandar Hemon

WORK

John, just home from work, asks me how my day was and I say that it was okay but that I didn't do any of my work because I was busy doing housework. Whose work is that? he asks, slyly.

I have just read an article in the *Times* about a white composer who is reaching new heights of productivity since embracing a dominant-submissive relationship with a black woman. He is the dominant partner, but his domination is not primarily sexual. His wife, who finds submission satisfying, attends to all his needs while he works at composing for fourteen hours a day.

At first, I don't understand why it is news that a man who has a woman doing all his housework is finding himself productive. But then I think: Maybe this is progress. Maybe what is news is that now we are calling this domination, when we used to just call it marriage.

John has never cleaned a toilet in our house, of this I am fairly certain. But I never take out the trash. We both wash dishes. The floors are an unclaimed territory, a no-man's-land. Neither of us cleans them for months at a time. Sometimes we hire a Polish woman to sweep and mop for us.

Molly doesn't think this is a good solution. You're just outsourcing the oppression, she tells me. She seems to be suggesting that the only ethical way to deal with housework is for all of us to clean up after ourselves. Or live in our own messes.

If you pay well and tip generously, Daryl argues, what's wrong with having someone else do the work? Isn't housecleaning, she asks, just like any other work? It seems not to be. The phrase "cleaning toilets" is shorthand for being demeaned. I know of a couple who hire a woman to clean their house, but not the bathrooms, because they think it's wrong to have someone else clean up their shit. Daryl and I are talking about this because our friend the immigration lawyer, who works fourteen-hour days, wants to hire a cleaning woman but her husband the public defender is against it on principle.

Well, then, cleaning their house should be his job, I suggest. But if a woman is going to do housecleaning, isn't it better for her to be paid than for her to do it free? Later, I rethink this. I could also say that prostitution is better than everyday bad sex, in that a woman is getting paid for something many women endure unpaid. But money is part of what makes sex work dangerous for women who don't want to be selling sex but have no other choice.

Which makes me wonder: does the woman who cleans my house sometimes, who doesn't speak English well and is trying to put a child through college, feel that she has any other choice? I've never asked her. The composer's wife does have a choice, this much I know. She once made her living as an administrative assistant in a bank, and she also founded a theater company. Her situation is feminist, she tells the *Times*, because she has chosen it freely, for her own pleasure.

I wonder if she thinks of what she is doing as work.

SERVICE

"It's a struggle to say, 'This is genuinely who I am,'" the composer's wife tells the *Times*. But, "To say I can't play out my personal psychodrama just because I'm black, that's racist."

Her name is Mollena Williams-Haas. Her pet name for her husband, who is Austrian, is Herr Meister. Mister Master. This strikes me as funny until, in a YouTube video of her speaking at a sexuality conference, I hear her refer to her husband as her "owner" and herself as his "slave."

In the video she appears with her husband, a mousy man. She does all the talking for quite a while, and when her husband begins to speak she adjusts the way he holds his microphone. She interrupts him. She corrects his imperfect English and clarifies what he means. She is brash and confident, and she doesn't fit my definition of submissive.

As if she knows what I'm thinking, she recounts a story about being told repeatedly that she wasn't very "slave-like." Having just accepted her own desire to be a slave, she found this painful. Her mentor, her "trainer," told her that if she wanted to be a slave, she must be quiet and she must be invisible. She should not call attention to herself or stand out. Hearing this, she thought, "I guess I'm not a slave." But then she met a woman who told her, "If your heart draws you to slavery and to service, go to it. Don't let anybody tell you what slavery means."

Maybe her true fetish, Lisa says, is irony. We're drinking wine on Lisa's porch and laughing about all this, about an inspirational speech devoted to owning your own slavery, but I'm seriously inspired. She just wants to be a slave on her own terms, I say, which is all I want out of my work, too.

Even before she was married, Williams-Haas had a contract with her husband that guaranteed her, among other things, health care coverage. Her contract also included a guiding principle drawn from BDSM: "It is the primary responsibility of the slave to protect the master's property at all times, up to and including protecting the property from the master."

My search for "race play" produces an article that profiles a Latino man who got into sex work because a clinic in his city was offering free health care for sex workers. He was an artist and he didn't have health insurance. He discovered, doing sex work, that some men wanted to use his body to play out racist fantasies. Before he became a sex worker, he was once traumatized when a lover used racial slurs during sex. But it was easier for him to accept this language in a "commodified exchange," which is, he says, a kind of drag, because "it was something I could put on and take off." He considers it a service to allow other men to exorcise their racist impulses on him.

Williams-Haas uses the word *service* with reverence. Her slavery might be play, but her service is real. Service, she maintains, can be erotic even when it has nothing to do with sex. "The sensations I experienced in the face of learning to properly serve formal [afternoon] tea," she writes, "felt a great deal to me like arousal." And here is where I begin to wonder if my own gravitation to service, what sometimes seems to be a pathological preference for unpaid labor, is itself a kind of kink. Or power play, maybe. I, too, find service satisfying. And satisfaction, as Williams-Haas notes, can be hard to come by.

—Eula Biss

STREETS OF FURY

W hen I was twelve, my big brother took me to a movie about boxers. It was called "Streets of Fury" or "Alleyways of Anger," something like that. It told the story of a skinny little kid who grew up in a tough neighborhood and became a boxer so he could pay the gambling debt his drunken father owed the mob. And how that kid fought—you had to see it to believe it. He charged at those who got into the ring with him with such fury that they didn't know what hit them. That's where the name of the movie came from, "Avenues of Rage" or "Roads of Vengeance," or whatever it was called.

A week after the movie, I took a bus to Jaffa, to a boxing club that was listed in the yellow pages, owned by some old Polish guy who claimed he was a former world champ. I didn't tell anyone about it. But I already had a plan. I would secretly train in the club every day until I was really good, and then I could get back at all the bullies in the neighborhood. Whenever they tried anything—bam!—I'd charge at them furiously, like the kid in the movie, and beat them to a pulp while all the girls watched.

It was a great plan, except that the trainer in the boxing club wouldn't sign me up. You're not for boxing, he said, you're a happy kid, go play soccer. I told him that he had to teach me, that boxing was my life, that I might look happy and normal, but I was full of rage and all I needed was a chance. He looked at me for a minute without speaking, and then took a pair of black boxing gloves out of his iron locker. He put them on my hands and led me into the ring, where I attacked all the bad guys from the movie and took them apart. Meanwhile, he left the club for a few minutes, and when he came back, he had a skinny black kid who looked Arab with him.

"You and him," the Polish world champ said, "no holds barred, no rules, three minutes." I was very glad he believed in me and was not only letting me fight during my first lesson, but with a kid even skinnier and smaller than I was.

Just as I was planning my hurricane attack, something smooth and painful hit my cheek. I was on the ground. A hot liquid was dripping down the left side of my face. Before I understood what was happening, he was on me, biting my shoulder like some kind of rat. Even more than it hurt—and it hurt a lot—it was frightening. I

17

began to cry and scream, but it didn't stop. A few seconds later, the Polish world champ came into the ring and separated us. "This is only your first lesson," he said as he sterilized my wound. "Come tomorrow, and I'll teach you the basics." I could tell from his voice that he knew I wouldn't come.

A year later, "Alleyways of Fury 2," or "Streets of Anger 2," whatever it was called, came to the movie theaters. This time, the hero was older, and he found another kid, an orphan whose parents had been killed by a drug dealer, and taught him how to box. Watching that orphan smash the face of a redheaded guy in a training bout made me feel a little sad that my parents had never been murdered when I was a kid, or even got drunk and beat me. Something, so I could have a little rage too.

—Etgar Keret
Translated from the Hebrew by Sondra Silverston

JAIME CORTEZ is a writer and visual artist based in Northern California. His fiction, essays, and drawings have appeared in diverse publications that include *Kindergarde: Avant-Garde Poems, Plays, Stories, and Songs for Children* (2103, edited by Dana Teen Lomax for Black Radish Books); *No Straight Lines*, a forty-year compendium of LGBT comics (2012, edited by Justin Hall for Fantagraphics Books); *Street Art San Francisco: Mission Muralismo* (2009, edited by Annice Jacoby for Abrams Press); and *Infinite City*, an experimental atlas of San Francisco (2010, edited by Rebecca Solnit for University of California Press). Jaime is currently working on a short-story collection.

The Nastybook Wars

JAIME CORTEZ

I

When you leave a grapefruit on a countertop for a couple of weeks, the membranes and fruity ligaments that hold together its pleasant rounded shape slowly weaken. Gravity insinuates itself, and the citrus's bottom begins a relentless downward migration. The underside spreads and takes on the flatness of the counter, while the top thins out. That defeated grapefruit shape was precisely the shape of Primitivo Doblado's head.

Primi, as everyone called him, was a summertime fixture in the sun-blasted garlic fields of Gyrich Farms. No one knew how he first arrived, or how the lucky bastard managed to get hired as a garlic topper summer upon summer, when better workers, younger, steadier, and more sober, were turned away by the literal truckload. Lacking a logical explanation, some of the workers attributed his good luck to forces from beyond the veil.

"How does he have the luck to get hired? I'll tell you how," my grandmother Tiburcia would rant. "In his wallet, that drunk, that stinking drunk, carries hairs from the ass crack of Satan himself. The luck of The Enemy is with him. You stay away from him, *hijo*."

Hollister's late summer heat was a dragon we feared and cursed daily when it swooped in around midmorning and hovered, heavy and relentless, till the evening hours. Because of the heat, the workday started early. Everyone was suited up by six. The men wore straw hats or baseball caps, and shirts with long sleeves they rolled down when their forearms began to roast around ten or eleven. The women were more covered up. They wore long-sleeved shirts and cotton gloves. Many of the younger women, protective of their skin, favored a sort of laborer's hijab from the shoulders up: a bandanna tied just above their eyebrows and back around their heads; a second, bandit-style bandanna over their nose and cheeks; and a third one to protect the back of their necks. Some wore a fourth one into which they coiled and bundled their long hair. All of this was topped off with a straw hat or baseball cap and held together by an elaborate array of bobby pins.

For me, my older sister Sylvie, my cousins, and other farm-working kids, summer was a dreaded season. The worst day of elementary school was better than the best day in the garlic fields. The garlic had been pulled by its long stems out of the soil in early August. Heaped along the furrows of the field for a week or two, it would begin to dry out and release a powerful garlicky aroma. The arid heat did its work, and once the garlic dried, it was ready for topping, which involved us cutting off the roots and stems with curved metal shears. Bone white, the stacked bulbs resembled mounds of tiny skulls curing in the sun and stretched out towards the edges of the Gabilan Mountain foothills, gold with tinder-dry grass.

Getting out of bed at sunrise was hard for us kids, but fueled by sunrise cups of Café Combate, beans, eggs, and supple home-made flour tortillas, we were ready to go. For Primi, getting to work on time was a grave burden and interfered with his drinking schedule. He almost never made the six a.m. start on time or sober. Didn't have good hands, either. Shaky. His stubby fingers were clumsy, wrapped in filthy white medical tape to protect the many cuts he had given himself with the garlic shears.

But he had bulldog magic, did Primi, that charm of the grotesque-but-benign. Quick to smile, boisterous, funny, but no fucking neck. Nada. His head, jowly and big-lipped like an Olmec idol's, sat squarely on his collarbones. To look to the sides, he had to turn his entire torso. Primi looked like what he was: a devoted beer guy. A riverine network of dilated capillaries marred his terra-cotta-colored cheeks. His beer gut jutted imposingly over his improbably scrawny legs. His voice was toad deep, loud, and gurgly, and the littlest kids out working in the field, the five- and six-year-olds, were visibly scared of him. I was equally scared and fascinated by his appearance, words, and almost aristocratic haughtiness and tantrums.

When Primi fell asleep on the toilet, a trio of young workers stopped their labor, grabbed a tow rope from their pickup, and wound it around the porta-potty, trapping him. Then they gathered around to laugh and throw dirt clods at the plastic walls. From inside, Primi began cursing in a stage voice. He was an improvisational prodigy, stringing together the most elaborate, rapid-fire passages of curses in English, Spanish, and Spanglish. In the torrent of invective, he bent "fuck" into every part of speech, firing it off as a noun, pronoun, verb, adverb, conjunction, and interjection. The madder he got, the louder he got, the more everyone laughed. When they finally let him out and he emerged, drenched in sweat, with his belt undone, everyone cheered. He looked about, bowed at the waist, and just like that, his anger evaporated.

He had no wife to enforce grooming. The more forensically inclined garlic toppers studied his queerly angled bangs and deduced that he

23

had been cutting his own oil dark hair with his garlic shears or perhaps a bread knife. At lunch, he ate like a twelve-year-old boy blowing his allowance—Laffy Taffy, Cheetos, pickled pig knuckles, Rainbo white bread sandwiches with triple baloney, double slices of government cheese, and peeking out from underneath the meatstuffs, representing the vegetable kingdom, what might once have been lettuce.

The days were long. To break up the monotony of topping garlic, I would rise from my stooped or kneeling position and treat myself to a long, luxurious, cone-shaped cup of water at the Igloo cooler. Others would gossip, joke around, or sing along to the lachrymose *rancheras* on their transistor radios. But of all the workaday distractions, none were so fascinating as the oracular musings of Primi. The workers would sporadically lob questions at him, and he would swat them back with élan.

"Primi, you wanna get married? Don't you wanna wife?"

He mulled over the question like an ascended guru.

"No, *ese*. I don't have money, so I can't attract someone better-looking than me. Imagine a woman with looks like mine. Sad, huh? Nope. *Chale*. No marriage. Besides, it's cheaper to rent."

"Primi, what's the best beer?"

"Whichever one is in my hand, *loco*."

"Primi, why do dogs love humans?"

"If you gave me free cans of meat and cleaned up my caca, I'd love you too, homeboy. Woof."

When Ligo and noticeably pregnant Chelo announced a late August wedding, they invited Primi and scores of the garlic crew, including us. The weddings of the poor are rarely poor. They function as working-class Oscar nights, rare avenues for glamour. The young women were unrecognizable out of their sun protection gear. Their hair, curled or set in fancy buns and braids, cascaded about their pale, exposed shoulders. Their painted lips left red marks on the lips of the plastic champagne flutes. The men went the opposite way, covering their darkened arms and necks. Their thighs and privates bulged against the snug polyester pants of the day, entrancing me.

Primi splurged and rented a ruffle-breasted shirt and matching maroon Bostonians. When he stepped into the San Juan Bautista VFW hall with a female escort, everyone whistled and catcalled. He took it all in like the pope, bowing his head slightly to the left, the right, and the center of the hall. He had arrived a bit drunk and quickly finished the job at the bar. Then he danced with his lady. She was young and sparkly, laughing and drinking like a champ at Primi's fevered pace. He was amped up with everyone's attention, jerking and shuffling about the dance floor like a troubled windup toy.

My *papi*, possessed of a spiked, alchemical genius for transmuting physical defects into nicknames, would periodically break into laughter as he watched Primi shake his beer boobs, and gyrate the sad bit of protoplasm he alleged was his ass. At some point that night, papi named no-neck Primi "Head and Shoulders." Everyone within earshot laughed. My mom, rosy-cheeked with champagne, halfheartedly checked my father. "Ai, leave Primi alone. That's how God made him." But it was too late. The name stuck. It had to stick, because it was perfect, slicing clean to the marrow of truth. Besides, papi had a christening reputation to uphold. He was gifted at nick-naming, almost synesthetic at times, able to come up with nonsense names that worked at the level of pure sound. Bucktoothed Chendo, with his voracious chewing patterns, became "Chaka Chaka." Pretty chubbette Rosalia became "Globulina." The Sinaloa shitkicker Gustavo became "El Quadrupero." Why he should be a quadruped we didn't know, but the name was undeniable, just like "Head and Shoulders."

The Monday morning after the wedding, the garlic topper guys were relentless, batting Primi's new nickname back and forth across the fields like a tennis ball. Some of the young men could barely pronounce his English nickname, but it was too delicious, too perfect, not to take a jab at Primi.

Head and Shoulders here.

Head and Shoulders there.

Head and Shoulders up.

Head and Shoulders down.

Until the novelty passed, it would have to be this way, and Primi knew it, so he just smiled through the ordeal, periodically insulting everyone's mother the way a game fellow should. When I called him Head and Shoulders to his face by accident, he actually laughed, bending down towards me and releasing a great cloud of beer breath into my face. I liked him for that. Not for the breath, but because he kept his cool. I was nine years old and was showing disrespect. He could have cussed me out, probably even smacked me for my insolence, not on the face, but upside the head, with full-throated approval from my parents.

Head and Shoulders' last day at Gyrich Farms came within a week of the wedding just as the garlic season was winding down. Two olive Immigration and Naturalization Service trucks and one van descended upon the garlic fields just before midmorning. They braked hard, kicking up clouds of dust and dirt clods.

"*La Migra, La Migra!*" shouted several garlic toppers. Six khakied INS agents exploded from the vehicles. It frightened me when several young workers bolted. The guys seemed so adult to me just seconds before, so full of bravado and that physical competence of young men, hefting heaping bushels of garlic onto their shoulders with thoughtless ease. In a moment, they had been stripped of that, and had been made into prey, fleeing to hide beneath cars or behind the garlic crates. I panicked and turned wide-eyed towards my mother.

"Should we run, *mami*, should we run?"

"What are you talking about? You're a citizen, born here. They can't take you away."

"What about you, *mami*? You were born in Mexico."

"No. I have my papers too," she said. "Now mind your own business and keep on working."

I watched the chase, and saw Head and Shoulders rise up slowly, calmly. He walked a few steps, then he began running. It wasn't even ten in the morning, but he had already downed two Coors tallboys, so he was wobbly. Dashing towards the cattails on the banks of the irrigation ditch, he tripped over a clod. Primi sprawled on the ground, arms and legs spread out like the Carl's Jr. star. His beer shot forth a geyser of foam, but amazingly, he never let that beer can go. An INS agent stood over him, then bent and grabbed Primi by the shoulder to help him stand. With his free hand, Primi sheepishly dusted himself off. He exhaled slowly, shoulders dropping and eyes turning dirtward as he emptied his lungs. He cast his eyes up, and caught mine. He winked and smiled a lopsided smile at me. Primi raised his beer can to his lips, tilted his head back, opened his throat, and poured in the pissy remains. Conspicuously pregnant Chelo cried silently as Head and Shoulders bent his back and entered the rear mouth of the INS paddy wagon.

Ligo tilted his head, sucked his teeth, and intoned, "Oh well, at least he got to finish his Coors."

The rest of the workday was somber and very quiet. The heat felt heavier than usual. There was hardly any chatter, and no one sang along with the transistor radio; there was just the metallic snip of shears slicing through garlic stems and roots, and the bonk bonk of the bulbs dropping into the bentwood bushel baskets.

II

That evening, Doña Sara, the foreman's wife, cleared out Head and Shoulders' tiny rental room in the high house. It was the only two-story building in the Gyrich Farms laborers' camp, with three little rooms on the ground floor, and three little rooms on the second floor. Tiny and identical, they all held mismatched, decrepit furniture: a wardrobe, a chair, a twin-size bed, and maybe a milk crate to serve as a night table. She packed his clothes into grocery bags in case he should make his way back across the border, but with it being so late in the season, she guessed he would wait a few weeks till the apple and pear harvests. She looked sadly at his undershirts, stiff and murky gray from bad washings with colored clothes, insufficient detergent, and not a whiff of fabric softener. "A man without a woman," thought Doña Sara as she Ajaxed his hot plate for the next tenant, "is a sad animal. Sad. Don't know how to take care of themselves. A wonder they know to reach around to wipe their own *culos*."

From behind the big willow tree that fronted the high house, my sister Sylvie and I, and my cousins Chucho and little Lola, spied on the cleaning with particular interest. Doña Sara put his radio, Sunday Stetson, coin jar, and a few other valuables into a box for safekeeping at her house. His remaining items were stuffed into garbage bags and placed in the wardrobe. As soon as she left and padlocked the door, we circled around to the back of the house. We studied the window. She hadn't latched it. Chucho punched through the rusted window screen and pried the window open with a screwdriver. We hoisted little Lola through the window and climbed in after her. We began rooting around, hoping to find a spare dime under the bed, or matches, or Mexican comic books, or candy, or maybe even cigarettes.

Sylvie opened the double doors of the rough-hewn wardrobe, and she and Chucho bent forward to examine the interior. They gasped simultaneously.

"Ooooooh! Oh my God! Oh my God! Oh my God!" squealed Sylvie.

"What is it?" I asked.

"Oh my good God!" added Chucho. Together they dragged out a grocery bag filled to the top with nasty girlie magazines. We swooped down on the bag, tearing it savagely as we reached in to pull out some porno. Each of us grabbed a handful and retreated from the others like a wolf with a deer leg.

"Ooooooh," I chanted from behind my copy of *Cheri*, "you can see her guts." I turned the centerfold around so everyone could see the eviscerated blonde.

"Thass not her guts, stupid," snarled Chucho, "thass her pussy." At twelve, almost thirteen, Chucho was the oldest, and our resident sexpert. Little Lola, aged only seven, was as confused as I was.

"How come iss all hairy?" she asked. Chucho had had enough.

"Stupid, you are a bonehead, Lola. Get out of here! This isn't for little kids." Chucho shoved her towards the window. Lola became teary-eyed and pleaded her case.

"I was just asking howcum iss all hairy, you don't have to throw me out."

"GET OUT, MONGOLOID!"

"I'm gonna tell mom," she threatened, her voice quavering. "And she, an' she, she's gonna hit you." Lola was a master snitch, and her mom was quite a hitter, so Chucho backed off.

"All right, then," Chucho agreed, "shut up and don't ask any more stupid questions."

"I'm just asking howcum it's all hairy, that's all."

"Look, little baby," said Sylvie with absolute eleven-year-old authority, "when women grow up they get hair. When you grow up, you'll get hair there too."

"No sir . . ."

"Yes sir. Matter of fact, your mom has hair down there. A big ol' spider bush."

"No sir," said Lola in a tone that was half denial, half question.

"It's not something you do, it just happens. Your mom has all kinds of hair. Probably down to her knees. Like it or don't." The revelation was too much for Lola. She began to wail.

"All right, that does it," said Chucho. "You girls get outta here. We gotta take these books and put 'em someplace safe."

"They're not your books, you know," countered Sylvie. "I was the one who opened the doors of the closet."

"But I saw them first," countered Chucho.

"But I touched them first, so we found them together, so they're everybody's."

"That's a good plan, there's thousands of them, and we can share," I offered.

"God, what kind of sissy idea is that?" asked Chucho. "Don't you get it, Jaime? What do the girls want them for? These books aren't for *girls*, they're for *men*!"

"You're not MEN," shrieked Sylvie, "You're just BOYS, and the girls wanna look at the pictures too!" Teary-eyed Lola nodded her head in agreement.

"These books belong to the boys," Chucho proclaimed. "And the boys are taking them."

"Yeah, the boys!" I added, eager to redeem myself as a dutiful foot soldier in Chucho's eyes.

S uddenly Sylvie grabbed an armful of magazines and made for the escape window. Chucho grabbed her by the pigtail and pulled her back into the room and they began to struggle, the two of them sliding on the glossy paper. Lola and I entered the fray and there ensued a tremendous ripping of paper, yanking of hair and center-folds, and opportunistic biting. The girls were scrappy, but they were dramatically outmatched. I was a big beefalo calf of a boy, and Chucho, while on the small side, rained down painful rabbit punches. In short order, the girls fled through the window and we latched it behind them. Sylvie, with a bit of crumpled centerfold still in her clenched fist, rapped on the window with her knuckles.

"Open the window! Jaime you know we should get to see them too!"

Red in the face and panting, I shouted back at her. "These are for BOYS, Sylvie. Go find your own dirty books for girls."

"There aren't any. So the boys have to share!"

Chucho put his face up to the window and brayed his evil laugh. Sylvie flipped him off with both hands, repeatedly stabbing the air with her middle fingers for emphasis. Little Lola tried to imitate the gesture, but flipped us off with her ring finger instead, sending me and Chucho into paroxysms of laughter.

"We'll be back, idiots! And we'll bring help!"

Chucho closed the curtains on Sylvie, and we collapsed on the floor, rolling around on our spoils. Chucho humped the floor lasciv-iously, kissed the centerfolds, and intoned, "Yes, yes, yessss!"

III

The giddiness passed. Chucho and I submerged ourselves in the pornography, oohing and ewwing and gasping as we flipped through the glossy pages. Dramatic tan lines, boobs of all sizes and shapes, masses of pubic hair, and out-thrust butts. It all seemed laughable to me, embarrassing to behold, until I saw a naked man in a couples photo shoot. I stared quietly, enthralled by his mustache and broad shoulders, alarmed by his pendulous pink scrotum and wild shock of ginger pubes. I memorized the cover of the magazine, knowing it would be my favorite. We finished our initial scan and organized the books into neat stacks. It was early evening by then. Tense and vigilant, I parted the curtains and peered into the encroaching twilight.

"I'm getting hungry, Chucho."

"You're always hungry, fatass."

"Time to eat, man. Let's get outta here now."

"Do you see the girls out there, Jaime?"

"Nope. I think they're gone."

"You know the plan, right?"

"Yes, Chucho. You only told me it a hundred times."

"Just checking. If you know it so good, tell me."

I sighed, and began reciting the plan.

"We fill that cardboard box with some of Head and Shoulders' junk. I go out the window with the box and pretend it's the nastybooks. I hide the box under the front porch stairs. The girls will see me and think they know our secret hiding place, but really they won't, because as a matter of fact, you'll have the real books in those pillowcases, sneak out when it's safe, and you'll hide the books in the tractor barn and tomorrow, we can look at the books some more after church."

"It's perfect," he hissed, shaking his head. "They'll never figure it out. Perfect."

I slipped out of Primi's window and Chucho handed me the box. I made a big show of pretending it was heavy with magazines. I lurched to the front of the high house, opening the little iron grill gate that led to the space under the stairs. I pushed the box through the opening and crawled in after it. As soon as I had disappeared beneath the stairs, I heard running footsteps. Through a crack in the stairs, I saw Sylvie and Lola. Shit.

"Ooh, Lola," said Sylvie theatrically, "there's something under the stairs. I think it's an animal."

"No it's not an animal, I think it's Jai—"

"Shut up, idiot! It's an animal. I think it was a pig. We'd better lock it in before it eats daddy's cucumber plants." Before I could scramble out from under the stairs, Sylvie closed the latch on the iron grill. She peered in and smiled as I struggled to force it open.

"*Que feo*! It's one of those big fat wild retarded pigs." I tried kicking the gate to no avail.

"You see how wild the pig is, Lola?"

"You better let me out, fucker!" I growled.

"Ooh, the pig is mad, but he better not get too mad, 'cause mami is right across the way in the kitchen and she'll come out if he makes too much noise, and she'll wanna know what you're doing down there, and we'll have to tell her all about the nastybooks."

I yanked at the gate but couldn't crack it open. I glared at her through the grill. She smiled serenely.

"You boys think we're stupid but we're not. I said I'd get help and I did. I got Big Cookie and she's on my team now."

"So," I said, "I'm not afraid of no Big Cookie."

"You looked pretty scared when she smacked you with her elbow and gave you a nosebleed."

"Well, I'm not afraid."

"Well, you should be. Right now, Cookie is kicking Chucho's ass and getting those books back. That's what you get for not sharing with the girls. And by the way, you guys are the fuckers, not us!"

"Big Cookie can't beat Chucho up. He's tough."

"She's taller, heavier, and even meaner than Chucho."

It was true. I had no retort. Sylvie turned and ran off towards the tractor barn. My heart was pounding so hard I could feel it in my temples. I lay on my side and tried to kick the gate open, to no avail. I crouched beneath the porch for what were probably a few minutes, but it felt much longer. Finally Sylvie returned and opened the latch. I sprang from the gate opening and tried twice to kick her, but she was rabbit fast and laughed at my failed efforts. I jogged to the tractor barn. There I found Chucho pinned stomach-down underneath Big Cookie, who was counting out loud, her fleshy lips slowly intoning each number.

"One hundred five. One hundred six. One hundred seven."

Big Cookie's ambush had clearly been rough. Torn scraps of nasty books were strewn about them. Chucho and Cookie were filthy from rolling around in the oily dirt of the tractor barn. Cookie had a little blood visible in her nostril. Chucho had a large scratch across his cheek and forehead. His shirtsleeve was torn. Big Cookie had thirty pounds on him. He never stood a chance.

"Get off him, Cookie," I said. Cookie turned to me coolly and sneered.

"You wanna help your boyfriend, Jaime?" she asked. "Well then, come on, and I'll smack you down too."

An unruly P.O.W., Chucho remained defiant.

"Those magazines are for men!" said Chucho.

"Not anymore," countered Big Cookie. "I beat you fair and square for them, Bozo. They're ours now, and we're taking them."

"You girls are stupid," said Chucho. "What do you wanna see naked girls for?"

"That's for me to know and you to find out. Now shut your hole and let me count to two hundred so I can finish your punishment and let you go."

"Fuckers," spit out Chucho.

"You guys are the fuckers," said Big Cookie. "If you had just shared, we would all have magazines and I wouldn't have had to rack you up. Now stop squirming, you idiot, or you'll never get outta here."

IV

For the next few days, the girls demonstrated how far in advance they were in the realm of psychological operations and manipulation. They led Chucho and me on a series of ranging, dead-end excursions. We'd spy the girls gathering behind the chicken coops and moving on purposefully to some unlikely place like the garbage heap or the inside of the abandoned Chevy that rusted away on the edge of the fields. There they would huddle tightly and converse, their eyes turned inward, backs obscuring their actions. Chucho and I would descend upon them with an "Aha!" only to find them empty-handed.

"Looking for something?"

"None of your business, Sylvie."

"Then why did you say 'Aha,' retard?"

". . . just because."

"You'll never guess where we put 'em, Chucho. You know why? Because you're dumb and we're smart. We might wait fifty or one hundred days before we even look at 'em. We're patience. Very very patience."

Their mocking laughter lashed us as we retreated. Entire days passed, and we saw no signs of activity. I was rapidly losing morale and interest, but reclaiming the books had become a point of honor for Chucho.

"Jaime, no matter what happens, we have to get those books back. I have a plan to get them."

"What's the plan?"

"Secret. But you gotta be in the plan or it doesn't work."

"What am I gonna do?"

"It's a secret, stupid. Just do what I tell you, no matter what. Will you obey?"

"Umm . . . okay."

"First we gotta find little Lola."

"I think she's over by the trailer."

"Good. C'mon."

As we approached, we heard Lola holding court at an alfresco tea party near a worker trailer in the garden. Kneeling in the dust, she was serving up mud pies and tin cans of water to her motley collection of rescue dolls. With their missing arms, hollowed-out eye sockets, scalped heads, and mismatched clothes, the dolls seemed to have crawled out of some horrible toy apocalypse, but Lola was a stellar hostess, making chatty conversation with them, and even serenading them with one of her patented fucked-up songs.

"Conjunction Junction, what's your fuck shuh? Lookin' at worse, and raisins in closets. Conjunction Junction, how's that fuck shuh? I got ants, button, or, they get you pretty far."

"Get her!" snapped Chucho. I pounced and grabbed Lola from behind.

"Lemme go!" she pleaded. She squealed and squirmed but quickly saw there was no hope of escape. Chucho assumed the role of inquisitor.

"Lola, where are the nastybooks?"

"I don' know."

"Don't be stupid, Lola. Tell us, or we'll make you suffer."

Less convincingly now, she repeated her denial. WHAM! Chucho slapped her across the cheek. We were all silent for a moment, shocked at what had just happened, trapped in an unfolding land-slide of events. Lola opened her mouth wide. She was one of those delayed howl kids who held their mouths open for eternities, sucking in great lungfuls of air before unleashing a deafening cry. I clamped my grubby hand on her mouth just as the prelude made its way up her throat. A fine thread of blood trickled from her left nostril, and I was quietly horrified.

"Chucho, this is too much, man. Don't hit her on the fa—"

"Shut up and stop being a pussy. She's going to tell me where the books are. Now where are they?" I removed my hand from her mouth.

"My nose," she cried.

"Where are they?" pressed Chucho.

"The books . . . the books . . ." she faltered.

"Spit it out!"

"They're in the old refrigerator," she sobbed, "by the ditch behind the High House."

"Let her go. Next time, you don't take our stuff, Lola."

"Maybe we will," she countered in a quavering voice. We were impressed by Lola's spunk but laughed anyway. The gods of war were with us again.

V

The nasty books were indeed stuffed into the meat and vegetable bins of the abandoned refrigerator. They smelled weird now, and many of the pages had tears, oily dirt, and footprints from the ambush in the tractor barn. Still, our joy was expansive as we repacked the storied booty into a burlap sack. We had only a few minutes to act before Lola rounded up the girls and found us. We grabbed a shovel from the tractor barn en route to the garlic field. There, we hid behind the mammoth wheel of a tractor and began digging.

"This plan is perfect, Jaime, they'll never find our books now," grunted Chucho as he shoveled.

"Yeah, perfect." We buried the now thoroughly distressed books and headed back to the toolshed. On our way, the girls intercepted us but said nothing. They stared at us, disgusted. We retreated, checking behind us all the way for some unexpected maneuver. It was eerie, that silence, those glares. Nothing happened, but it felt so ominous. Any act of vengeance was possible now.

At home that night, I showered and drank my usual nightcap, chocolate Pancho Pantera mixed with milk. But I could not sleep. In the bunk above mine, Sylvie lay silent. I knew she was awake. I felt her contempt radiating through the bottom of her bunk, cooking me from the inside out like a microwave.

"You asleep?" I asked. She said nothing. I lay in the dark and breathed as softly as I could and pondered how to fix the heavy damage I'd inflicted on my relationship to my sister, Lola, and Cookie. I drifted off to sleep, enveloped in the malignant, suffocating quiet.

The next day was a Saturday. Normally it was the best day of the week. Sylvie and I would watch early cartoons and wait for Mom to treat us to our weekly pancake breakfast. I asked Sylvie if she wanted to watch cartoons, and she said simply, "No." I watched my favorite, *Scooby-Doo*, but it wasn't much fun on my own. All morning Sylvie maintained monastic silence. By lunch, Mom had become curious.

"Why are you two quiet?" she asked.

"It's nothing. Just don't feel like talking," said Sylvie.

"Don't tell me it's nothing. If you're not chattering, something's wrong."

"I'm finished eating," said Sylvie. "Can I go now?"

"Yes, but if something happened, you should tell me."

"No, nothing serious. Me and Jaime, we had an argument, that's all."

Our war had escalated and taken on its own momentum. I didn't really care about the books anymore. I don't know if anyone did. It was now a war for the honor of the boys or the girls. I was a sissy boy, and that binary was excruciating to me. I wanted to tell Sylvie where the books were, but that would show Chucho I wasn't a real boy. Surely he would sever my tenuous connections to the world of boys. Surely I would be exiled to the world of girls, and surely they would send me away too. Troubled for yet another night, I counted sheep in the dark. Then horses. Deep into a chicken count, I finally fell asleep.

For three days, we let the books lie in the soil of the fallow tomato field. Troubled though I was, I still found it delicious to exchange conspiratorial glances with Chucho, knowing the girls were baffled, knowing the dirty books lay in the soil like fleshy seeds. On the fourth day, shortly past six a.m., a tiller tractor made its first pass over the field and the box of nasty books. All morning long, it criss-crossed the field, its great steel disks cleaving the soil, breaking it into ever smaller clods with each pass. The dirty books did not fare well, and by the time we'd awoken and stepped outside, we could only watch helplessly from the edge of the field, knowing that the tiller had sliced the magazines into slivers. Late summer breezes kicked up dust and centerfold remnants.

My grandma Tiburcia emerged from her kitchen to use the out-house. On her way there, she saw a pink scrap of centerfold. She picked up the scrap of photo and looked at it with narrowed eyes. It took a moment, but she deciphered it. *"Ave Maria por encima,"* she whispered under her breath. She looked about in alarm. Scraps everywhere. The devil was hard at work, but she knew just what to do. Grandma got her neighbor Doña Paquita to help her round up all of us kids into her living room and quarantine us. Then she and Doña Paquita ran out like fussing hens, chasing down every scrap they could find and tossing it into a paper sack. The disposal of our pornography was perfunctory and largely unlamented by the kids. We were war-weary and ready for new diversions.

For weeks afterward, scraps missed by Grandma would appear in corners—bits of tit, snatches of snatch, hanks of hair, and bouquets of tightly clenched toes that skipped along the dusty labor camp. After Grandma threw out the bag of picture scraps, Big Cookie salvaged it, and she instructed the kids to grab all the scraps of porno we found and collect them in a weathered cigar box that would serve as a reliquary. Periodically, we would open the box, lay the pieces out on a tabletop, and study them with Talmudic intensity. We wanted to piece together an enticing nude, but instead we assembled grotesque Frankenforms with outsize lips, mismatched limbs, and demented eyes that elicited more giggles than gasps of wonder. We didn't have all the pieces, but we were united again, a secret order of kids bent on piecing together an incomplete puzzle from the lurid, enticing world of grown folk.

TRACY K. SMITH is the author of four volumes of poetry, including, most recently, *Wade in the Water*, and *Life on Mars*, which won the Pulitzer Prize. Her memoir, *Ordinary Light*, was a finalist for the National Book Award in nonfiction.

The Pack of Wolves and the Family of Dogs

TRACY K. SMITH

When I hear my name, a campfire lights inside me and I can tell she is pacing around in her coat, sticking her head in all the rooms, asking herself where can I be. I run to the backside of the house, behind the spiky bushes splotched with bird berries. I stab the toe end of my shoe into the ground at the pine needles and dry leaves and the red berries until I make a dark hole.

A good stick would do it, but I can't get there with a shovel. If I dig with a shovel, I'll end up with a garden or a grave. What I'm looking for might be only as thick as a grain of rice standing up on one end, but when I find it, it'll open up into a whole realm or else I'll become exactly the right kind of small. It has its own sky and sea and cities. It's like another earth, only different.

When my clothes fill up with heat I spread my arms and run another loop through the frosty air. There goes my name again, like a flag my mother is waving. Like she is on the ground and I am coming in for a landing. In all the stories about being lost, it's the kids who roam away and get scared. But in real life sometimes the kids stay put and the parents wander off. I cover the hole with leaves. I flap the bottom of my shirt to let the cold air all the way inside, then I run out and slap the side of the car like we are playing a game of tag and that is home. When my mother sees me, her forehead gets pinched. Get in the car, she says, we're going to be late. I wish she would open her coat and let some of her heat out, but she won't. I squish into the backseat between my brothers and click the buckle into the slot so Mom doesn't boil over. If I am ever lost, I will be right under her feet.

Sebastian yanks my hair. He's the bigger one. Sometimes he gets mad and throws his sippy cup so it crashes and the milk splats everywhere. When he does that, my mother's eyes close and her chest heaves once like she is concentrating on a math problem. Now, she looks only at me in the mirror and asks what I did to him. I didn't do anything! I was just sitting here and he pulled my hair for no reason. Mom says, Sebastian be nice, but not in the voice she uses when I do something bad. My spirit starts to spin very fast. It scrapes up every bit of feeling I have inside me and howls it into the air of the car. The sound is long and rough and angry and sweet. To me it sounds far away, like it is charging across time to before when we were still wolves. Stop that! she yells. Her voice is jagged, like it has been dragged over rocks. And then, Sorry Sweetheart. Tell me something you're learning about in school.

I tell her Greek mythology. Mythology is what religion becomes after the people stop believing in it. She asks, Who's your favorite god? Her eyes find me again in the mirror. She uses her hand to smooth away the dents in her forehead. I tell her Hades. Really? Hades? She doesn't say anything after that. The crossing guard lifts up his sign and we have to stop.

School is okay. Last year my teacher was so beautiful I dreamed of her standing beside the bathtub with a fluffy towel stretched wide to wrap me in. Last year I loved Victoria and I got mad when we played Castle and she chose Nikhil as king and I was just a knight. Last year Cedric and I had to be separated for saying bathroom words and my mother asked me to leave the boys alone and play with the other girls. But girls only want to play tame things. Even when we play Castle the girls are the ones standing still while all the rest of us race into battle against enemy armies. Cedric punched me once. Once, I climbed almost all the way to the top of the tallest tree and my heart was like a fish that had been lifted out of a lake and carried through the air just under the clouds the way I've seen a bird do.

At recess, everything is boys or girls. Boys chase each other with sticks and get dirt caked in the lines of their hands. Girls whisper to each other and chase you with their eyes. Before my mother had boys she was the queen wolf and my father was the king wolf and I was the little wolf cub. When we were a pack of wolves my mother taught me to hunt. She taught me to whine and growl when danger lurked. We stood in the night watching for deer. We wrestled together in the tall grass and sniffed at tracks in the moonlit snow. Now my family is a family of dogs but I am still my old self. I am losing all my young teeth and soon I will be fierce. Now that my mother is a dog she lies on the rug and covers her nose with her tail. She lifts her head when my brothers yelp, and rolls over to let them drink her milk.

In math, Emma's face gets red and she starts shaking. I know she is about to cry. It's just like Emma to cry about how many nickels Peter should get back if he uses a quarter to buy a piece of candy that only costs ten cents. I whisper her the answer but my teacher hears and says, Rosalind this is a test. Turtles don't have ears but they can hear. Even a red-eared slider doesn't have ears you can see. The earth turtle is an imaginary species. An immortal jellyfish turns back into a baby when it gets scared. It can only die if another animal eats it. Some plants eat meat.

At lunch I try to eat without hands. I dip my chin down to the tabletop and shoot my eyes to Cedric on the left and Nikhil on the right in case I need to be ready to bare my teeth. Sometimes I want to live on the ground, on all fours, wriggle on my back with my arms and legs in the air. I am just swallowing when Victoria points and says, Look at Rosalind eating like an animal! Ooh, like a dog, says Kelsey. Kelsey is chubby with an oldish person's face. I curl my lip and growl at them with only my eyes. You don't know the first thing, my eyes say. And it's true, they don't. They can't recognize how close they are to danger. Here doggy, Victoria says, holding up a goldfish. Here doggy, Kelsey says, but she's too greedy to risk losing even one tiny morsel of her lunch, so she only snaps her fingers. Soon everyone at our table is laughing and I'm sitting there scowling at them all, not a wolf anymore except on the inside.

Up here, it's hard to be my whole self. But in the underworld, if you want to snarl like a beast with three heads, no one thinks it's unusual. In the underworld there's space for a kid who nobody knows what she is.

When she picks me up after school, my mother has a tired look, like something she wanted fell on the floor and rolled under the middle of her bed and she has been trying to reach for it all day with just one arm. My brothers are just where I left them except now they're eating chocolate cookies. Even before I'm all the way in the backseat I say, Hey that's not fair, where's my cookie? I know my mother hears it like a high-pitched whistle that pierces her ears. Her chest heaves. I see her go over the math problem in her mind. She says, Calm down, I have your cookie right here. But of course before I'm done with it Sebastian is crying for more. He's screaming, 'Bastian wants a cookie treat! And then Dexter starts in for no reason except that he's a twin so he has to if Sebastian does. I know my mother is going to say it, but I think maybe she won't this time, and then there it is. Break them off a couple of bites, Roz Sweetheart, it's a big enough cookie.

I n the underworld, the monsters are just as terrible as the ones here, but if you're brave you can lead them around on a leash. Everything you feel up here is dimmer in the underworld because all the color is drained away.

M om wants to know what else about my day but I can't decide what to say, what I did, or what I thought. I don't know, I tell her. It was just a day. Mine too, she says. Just a day. We go to the park. My brothers scramble out of the stroller and race to the sand-pit. Mom pushes me on the swings and I try not to pump my legs so she won't stop. I like her warm hand on my back, like when it was just us and her eyes weren't always combing through the distance making sure my brothers can't escape. A plane zooms overhead, tracing a white cloud through the sky like a dream that starts to vanish even before it's done.

A nother little kid wanders into the sandpit with her mother. Her mom scoops a shovelful of sand and sprinkles it into the little kid's hands. Then the kid dumps it out and they do it again and again. Each time the kid laughs and the kid's mom pretends to get frustrated. I guess some moms only pretend to get frustrated. The kid laughs and laughs and then runs around the sandpit asking to be chased. When Dexter and Sebastian put down their dump trucks

47

and join the game Mom stops pushing me and says, Maybe we should go check on your brothers.

I want to disappear down into the underworld for just a few months at a time, like Persephone. I want my mother to know what it's like to be abandoned.

It starts to turn dark. In the car, my brothers point at all the flashing traffic lights: Green! Yellow! White! Red! Red! Red! I ask Mom why children can be raised by wolves but not the other way around and she tells me it's just a figure of speech. I ask her who teaches animals how to take care of their children and she tells me they do it out of instinct.

We pass a family of deer that stands by the road watching like we're a very brief parade.

At home, my brothers jump on beds while dinner cooks. They pile pillows on the floor and cover them in a quilt. They take off their diapers and stomp naked down the hall. Through the back windows, the last stripe of daylight floats above the ground behind our trees. Wind runs circles through a mountain of leaves.

She doesn't hear the back door when I go out. I find the spot from this morning and start in first by kicking at the dirt with my feet. It's like a dance I'm doing in a circle, stabbing at the ground with my toes, driving through the dirt until I've carved out a bowl I can stand in to my ankles. Then I drop down to my knees and keep digging. The dark dirt sticks to my hands like clay and for the first time all day I get cold. I have to stop and pull my sleeves down past my fingers. I get up and run to the dark edge of the yard, to where the deer hurry back to when we startle them. Branches and twigs.

The last sliver of orange red light at the bottom of the sky about to disappear.

Through the back windows I can see my brothers fighting over a truck. Sebastian hits Dexter, then Dexter throws himself down to the floor. He is so angry he does it twice. Throws himself down, gets up, and throws himself down again.

I'm getting somewhere now with the forked end of a stick. I'm getting to the point where maybe I could sit down and wait to see if anything comes. Instead, I jab one more time hard at the dirt and all at once the bottom drops out of the hole. The dirt falls down into itself like the world is flat and I've dug straight through to the other side.

Squinting, I can see a cluster of furry bodies turning circles in the hole. Then they go stiff like stuffed dolls. Their black eyes look up at me and I can't help staring back. We stay frozen like that. I feel the weather pick up inside me and my veins go loud with thunder but I don't run. Then the big fat one, the queen woodchuck, stands. She says something I can almost understand in my bones, something urgent. She tells me, No. Or she tells me, Wait. Then they disappear through a passageway in the earth.

Rosalind! Mom's voice leans out from the doorway and the porch light obeys. Rosalind! It's a yell now, a spear she launches out that comes back empty. Rosalind? Now she says it like there may be no answer to the question.

When I was small, she'd tuck herself around me and nuzzle her chin in my fur. She smelled like rain and earth, and when she breathed the whole world heaved. I'd bury my nose in her. If she ran

49

in her dream, I ran too. Our paws twitched. Barking sounds echoed in our throats. I think the world was younger then. Before fear. Before everything. When we closed our eyes, another life switched on. I don't know if it was inside this one or underneath it. Now, when I sleep, she tiptoes back out into the kitchen. Under her clothes, there is nothing but skin.

I get in trouble for tracking in all that dirt, and for the hole Mom walks out to investigate in the yard. I have to take a bath before dinner. When I come back into the kitchen, my brothers have already been fed. Dad is on his back on the living room rug soaring them like airplanes with his feet.

Mom stands beside me while I brush my teeth but her eyes are looking at something only she can see. I want her to sit up in her bed at night and send her spirit out in every direction trying to find me. I want her to crawl on her knees and cover the yard with tears that harden into ice. I want these things so badly I am scowling and my body is clenched tight like a fist. Something like electricity is coming out of me and I want her to touch me so she'll feel the shock.

Oh Roz Honey, look at you. She smiles at us in the mirror. Look at you, Sweetie. You're like a, like a—. But she doesn't say like what. In the next room Dad is reading something singsongy to my brothers. I hear his voice bobbing up and down like a bouncing ball and their laughter chasing after when the ball dribbles out.

Come on, Sweetie. She leads me by the hand and lies down beside me in my bed. Lie down, my fierce little pup. She tucks herself around me and kisses me on the head. I feel our old life come close. It recognizes us but then it backs away. Something has vanished from our scent. It doesn't trust us anymore. We lie still a long time.

I hear the silent mischief of the foxes and the owls and raccoons. I hear the cold air climbing down from the moon and covering the ground with fog.

When I find the woodchuck tomorrow she'll see I'm meant for there and won't say no. She'll take me to a river and a boat and stand waving me off from the bank. Aboveground my mother will howl for me day after day as winter sets in. Smoke will scribble messages in the sky that I'll send up an unforgiving wind to erase.

AMINATTA FORNA is the Windham-Campbell Prize-winning author of the memoir *The Devil That Danced on the Water*, which was short-listed for the 2003 Samuel Johnson Prize. Her novels include *Ancestor Stones*; *The Memory of Love*, winner of the 2011 Commonwealth Writers' Prize for Best Book; *The Hired Man*, which was chosen as one of the best books of 2013 by National Public Radio and the *Boston Globe*; and *Happiness*. Forna's books have been translated into sixteen languages. She is currently the Lannan Visiting Chair of Poetics at Georgetown University.

Walking

AMINATTA FORNA

PRETTY GIRL

I am twenty. I am walking along the King's Road in Chelsea in London. It is the nineteen-eighties. Three men are coming towards me; they are clearly together, though the foot traffic on the pavement requires each to walk a half pace behind the other. They are white, dressed in tight jeans and cap-sleeve T-shirts. The first man, as he passes, looks me in the eye and says: 'You're a pretty girl.' The second one smirks, but says nothing. The third one leans into my face and breathes: 'Nigger!'

My final year at university and I had a part-time job working for an American foreign correspondent. One of my tasks was to pick up the broadsheets each morning, and in those pre-Internet days I would leaf through them and clip and file any articles on the stories he was covering. That day was a Saturday in summer. I generally came in later on the weekend and the street was already busy with people. I was on my way to his house with my haul of newspapers when I passed the three men.

You're a pretty girl.

Nigger.

The first remark did not seem designed to offend. You're a pretty girl. It intruded on my thoughts, got my attention. Then came the complicity of the second man. Then, 'Nigger!' What happened afterwards? Do you imagine that the first man berated the third man? Do you think they argued? And whose side did the second man take? None of that happened. I know it didn't. You know it didn't. The three men carried on walking down the road. At some point one of them likely turned to the others.

And they laughed.

WALKING

A child learns to walk. The child hauls herself up on a chair or her mother's knee, finds her balance and takes one tottering step and then another. The parents murmur sounds of encouragement, spread their arms. Come! Come! The father catches the child and swings her up in the air. My mother tells me that my approach was a little different from most infants'. I would crawl into the empty middle of the room and there I would take a breath and slowly rise. And I used my growing independence not to run towards her but to run gleefully away.

I grew up in the compounds of developing countries, in West Africa, where my father was from; and Southern Africa, the Middle and Far East, where my stepfather's career as a diplomat took us later. The hazards of the compound were snakes mainly, and army ants. As children, my brother, my sister and I didn't leave the compound alone much except to go and buy sweets or when we broke out in search of adventure. Around the age of five I began to borrow my brother's clothes. Boys' clothes afforded a greater practical freedom, were better for sliding down banisters, climbing trees, even the simple act of sitting. There was a lot of focus when I was growing up on making sure I sat properly, that is with my legs closed. My brother didn't have to sit that way, which seemed odd to me, given that he had something far more prominent to display. I wondered why, if what girls had between their legs needed to be so closely guarded, we were the ones to wear skirts.

I went to boarding school at six and left at eighteen for university in London. The enclosed worlds of compound life and British boarding school left me unprepared for the streets of the capital, the act of walking, specifically of walking alone and female down a street. Yet in my tomboy/cross-dresser days, which lasted until I was around fourteen, I had already begun to understand viscerally something I couldn't articulate. I didn't want to be a boy; I wanted the freedom I saw belonged to boys but not girls.

2017. I am standing on the platform of a London tube station, I'm back in the city where I lived for thirty years, before making my home in the United States. A young man is looking at me. I ignore him, but his stare is intrusive. When we board the train he stands very close to me, and at one point his hand touches mine. I am twice as old as him, which makes this situation somewhat unusual. But everything else about it is familiar, and I'm old enough now to recognise exactly what is going on. The next stop is mine and so I move to stand facing the door. He follows and stands right behind me; I can feel his breath on the back of my neck. The train is crowded, it's unlikely anyone else has followed his behaviour closely enough to think it out of line. What the young man doesn't realise is that I am facing the wrong door. This is my old home station, and the doors behind us will be the ones to open. At the last moment I swing round and exit.

A week or so later, on the tube again, I catch the eye of a man sitting opposite me. For a few moments I hold his gaze and then I look away. In the moment of turning I see him smile and it is a smile of triumph. He has won something, he has defeated me. Like the first man he is very young, around twenty. In that moment I realise something chilling. My God, I thought, he's *practising*.

Nobody tells young girls that men own the power of the gaze. My mother never told me that men may look at me but I may not look back. That if we do our look can be taken as an invitation. Men teach us that. Over the years we train our gaze to skim men's faces, resting for only a split second, shifting fractionally sideways if our eyes happen to meet. The man on the other hand, if he so wishes, will look at your face, your breasts, your legs, your ass.

In her 1975 essay 'Visual Pleasure and Narrative Cinema,' Laura Mulvey described how films are created to be seen from the point of view of the heterosexual male. Their female characters are presented to him as objects of desire. This is the 'male gaze.' The gaze is power. Men own the power of the gaze. White people do, too. A white friend tells me of the time she took her adoptive daughter who is black to a small town in Maine and found her daughter the object of stares. 'I guess there aren't too many black people in that part of the country,' she suggests placatingly, because already I am visibly irritated. 'And they don't own a fucking television?' I say. 'And they've never laid eyes on their president or his family?' (This was early 2016.) They stare because they can, by the gift of the power vested in them by their membership in the ethnic majority. They stare because her daughter's discomfiture is nothing to them, may be the whole purpose.

When a man stares at a woman in public her sensitivities are, at the very least, immaterial to him. He owns the power of the gaze and he will, if he cares to, exercise it. The real mind-fuck is that enfolded into the action is the defence. The woman who complains may well find herself being told she should be flattered, that she is lucky men find her attractive.

'Where you going, baby?'

'Smile, little lady.'

'Sssssss!'

'Want some of this?'

'Look at the ass on that!'

'You wouldn't be able to walk if . . .'

''Til . . . it . . . bleeds.'

In the early nineties I shared an apartment in London's Chelsea with a friend. One week, while repairs to the roof were being undertaken, we had scaffolding erected at the front of the house. My room was on the top floor and faced the street, and from there I could see the roofers go up and down the ladders. At certain times throughout the day they would take their breaks sitting on the scaffold deck right in front of my desk unaware that I could hear them as they took turns yelling comments at the women passing in the street below. The excitement each opportunity provoked was astonishing. 'Here comes one, here comes one! Your turn!' One man in particular was actually jumping up and down on the scaffolding. The more evidently humiliated the woman, the greater the delight. From where I sat I noticed several things: Firstly, yes, the young and attractive women drew more aggressive attention, as if the men were intent on denigrating what they could not possess, to punish the woman for being desirable and also unobtainable to them; secondly, no woman who was walking alone was exempt; and thirdly, they especially liked to pick on women who were dressed for work, who almost certainly earned more than they did. The women were metaphorically stripped, just as women were in earlier times and still are publicly stripped in some parts of the world, for transgressing the boundaries of womanhood, for stepping out of their place. They were being shamed, stripped not of their clothing, but of their dignity.

As a child I was taught to ignore aggressive dogs, to keep walking. Once you're out of its territory, the dog will leave you alone, so goes the conventional wisdom, and mostly it works. The same is supposed to be true of men, except it isn't. They walk alongside you, they kerb-crawl you. If you tell them to leave you alone they will call you a bitch and ask you who the fuck you think you are. Every encounter, however seemingly benign, contains the possibility of violence. By the time it is over (you have entered a shop or a subway), your breath is coming quickly and your heart slamming against your ribcage. Why do men do this? Nobody asks the question and when I ask, I don't get an answer. Sometimes it is said or suggested that this is simply the nature of men. What is interrogated more often is my response. Submissiveness is what is demanded. Women are taught not to answer back, for if we do we will escalate matters and then—the subtext—whatever follows will be our own fault.

Except I do, I do answer back. For, you see, it is in my nature.

In London in those early years, I get into fights. In South Kensington a man threatens to punch me after I tell him to piss off. I say I am going to fetch a policeman and if he is still there I will have him arrested. He swears at me, but he goes. A man in Camden Town pulls out a knife and threatens to stab me in the stomach. A crowd, mostly white, gathers around me and watches to see what will happen. The man is black and so am I. The stand-off goes on for long seconds. 'Do you want to fuck with me? Do you want to fuck with me?' Even then the ghost of a joke crosses my mind. Well, I thought I'd made it perfectly clear. Another man, also black and wearing dreads, moves through the audience. He walks up to us both, looks at the man with the knife and says: 'What's the problem, brother?' I never see that man again, not even to thank him, because the friend with whom I am walking has found a policeman and my harasser flees. But he is caught, and he goes to court and I am there, and I see him. His hair is braided and he wears a shirt and suit; he looks so different I wonder if I would have picked him out of a line-up. My statement is read to the court. He is found guilty, not of the sexual harassment which began the whole altercation, although the judge tuts at this part of my statement, but of possession of an offensive weapon. The case is over in minutes, my assailant is sent away to be sentenced at a later date. The girl I was walking with and her father attend the case. They both make it clear, though not unkindly because I have now learned my lesson, that this is my fault.

Later, when I tell the story I will discover that in the eyes of many of my white friends, the fact that I am black and both my harasser and saviour are black makes this a 'black thing.' Something in which they have no stake and in which the mostly white onlookers are now exempt from interfering; the courage of the dreadlocked man is suddenly not so great.

On the streets race and gender intersect, the dominance of men over women, of white over black, of white men over white women, of black men over black women, of Hispanic men over Hispanic women and so forth. Layered upon that is the relationship between men, the sometime competition and sometime complicity between men of all colours, the upholding of male power. This can play out in a variety of ways. For a woman of colour, men of the same ethnicity may be ally or foe.

In London men view street harassment as an equal opportunities occupation. I've endured sexually aggressive behaviour from men of every colour and class. In New York I am rarely publicly bothered by white men. How to account for the difference? In America the edges of racial politics are sharper and more bloodied. Human motivations are often hard to fathom, but I'd give a good guess that white men in New York City are scared to be seen harassing a woman of colour. To be *seen*. In *public*. There is also this—that within the codes of heterosexual masculinity, black men have ownership of and therefore power over black women. In some places this code is more strictly enforced than in others. On one of my last visits to the city I had to pass a group of workmen on a narrow sidewalk as they stood leaning with their backs against a building. In London this would be an inescapable moment. But we were in New York. All the men were white except one black man at the end. I was dragging an overnight bag and so my progress was slow. The men went silent and watched me as I passed. The unspoken rule, I sensed, was that the job of calling out to me belonged to the last man, the black man. I walked towards him and it seemed we both knew what the other was thinking. Would he betray his race or his place in the patriarchy? As I passed he leaned forward and, audible only to me, whispered: 'I like your jacket.'

Emmett Till was murdered. Emmett Till did not own the power of the gaze, at least not as far as Carolyn Bryant was concerned. Fifty-plus years on, white women friends in New York complain of the behaviour of some black guys there. They worry about being thought racist if they complain. This is the power play between men, the revenge exacted by certain black men upon white women but in reality upon white men. Payback is the pickup truck bearing a Confederate flag that cruises me twice on a long, lonely run in Western Massachusetts, the white guy with the baseball cap who turns his head and licks his lips on each pass.

#NOTALLMEN

At some point most women come to the silent and terrible realisation that the men in their lives—fathers, brothers, uncles, boyfriends and husbands—are not especially outraged by their experience of sexual harassment.

Late one evening when I was in my mid-twenties I had a row with my then-boyfriend. I decided to go home until I remembered the time of night, that I didn't have a car and would have to call a taxi if I hoped to execute my walk-out. I had very little money at the time and I'd have to weigh the cost of the taxi against the level of my outrage. A few months later, arguing with the same boyfriend (things didn't last too much longer) while on holiday in Southern

France, I remained walking on one side of the road while he crossed to the other. We were headed for the beach and the road was more or less empty. A man driving by, assuming I was alone, began to proposition me. I ignored him for a few moments and then I told him to get lost; finally I crossed to walk with my boyfriend and the man drove away. I remember very well my boyfriend's reaction. He laughed at me.

Writing about South Africa, where the incidence of rape is among the highest in the world, the feminist activist, poet and academic Helen Moffett has stated: 'Under apartheid, the dominant group used methods of regulating blacks and reminding them of their subordinate status that permeated not just public and political spaces, but also private and domestic spaces. Today it is gender rankings that are maintained and women that are regulated. This is largely done through sexual violence, in a national project in which it is quite possible that many men are buying into the notion that in enacting intimate violence on women, they are performing a necessary work of social stabilisation.'

In other words, rapists are the shock troops of male power.

The more I think about it, the more I come to the uneasy conclusion that, whilst #notallmen are rapists or sexual harassers, equally #notallmen are too unhappy about the status quo either. The relative vulnerability of women in public spaces limits our freedom of movement and our choices. Good practise in personal safety—telling someone where we are going, allowing ourselves to be escorted home and not walking alone at night—all add up to an effective form of social control. 'The necessary work of social stabilisation.'

Only in the second half of the twentieth century did middle-class women in many Western countries acquire some degree of freedom outside the home; before that, to walk unaccompanied was to be taken as a prostitute, a 'woman of the streets,' a 'streetwalker.' Walking, for a woman, can be an act of transgression against male authority. When a man walks aimlessly and for pleasure he is called a flâneur; a certain louche glamour attaches to the word. One rarely hears the term flâneuse. In her account of women walkers, itself called *Flâneuse*, Lauren Elkin observes that: 'narratives of walking repeatedly leave out a woman's experience.' Historically the free-ranging woman who dispensed with the domestic to claim ownership of the streets was a rare creature. Virginia Woolf, Jean Rhys, George Sand, the flâneuses who recorded their flânerie were women who all defied male authority in other ways, too. George Sand wore male dress so that she could move more freely around Paris.

Only once has a man ever stood up for me against harassment by another man (with the exception of the dreadlocked man, though he did not know what had started the trouble) and the man who did so was gay. We were standing outside a bar in Soho in London smoking cigarettes when a young man passed me and made a remark to which I responded with a put-down. His rage was instantaneous. He was smoking too and he threatened to burn me with his cigarette, holding the lit end close to my cheek. My companion intervened and in doing so drew fire away from me, literally because now the burning cigarette tip was being held to his neck. The scene ended when a friend of the assailant pulled him away. Afterwards we talked about it. I observed that a straight man would almost certainly have reprimanded me for my comment but he, notably, had not. No, he told me, because he grew up having much the same fight on the streets: the sexual insults, the shouted provocations. As a gay man he had learned to stand up to bullies.

Yet when I have talked to straight men about what happens to me on the streets I have consistently been met with looks of blank innocence. They insist they know nothing of it. I have seen the same conversation played out extensively on social media where the men most devoted to the use of the hashtag #notallmen always claim ignorance, are 'surprised,' so 'surprised' they'll go as far as to insist that what women are telling them cannot possibly be true, that invention or exaggeration on a global scale must surely be in play. Talking to a straight man about street harassment can be, as many black folk including black men have pointed out, like talking to some white people about the daily indignities of racism.

Somehow something enacted in broad daylight thousands of times in the lifetime of virtually every woman has gone entirely unnoticed by most straight men. At some point you have to ask: How can it be so?

How can it be so?

ON MATRIARCHY

I am driving down the road from my home in Freetown when a youth makes a kissing noise at me. I brake hard, bringing the car to a halt. 'Did you hear that?' I ask the friend I have with me. She says she did. 'I don't believe it,' I tell her. To the young man I say: 'Come here!'

I expect this kind of behaviour in many places, but I have not experienced it in the city where I spent many of my formative years. The youth, in his late teens or early twenties, is leaning against a wall in the company of four or so friends. One of them nudges him and points to me, telling him he is being called. He pushes off the wall and approaches the car; he saunters over but his cockiness has already lost its edge. People are watching, not just his mates but the women stallholders on the other side of the road. A couple of passersby, too, have stopped.

As I have said, I grew up in several countries in the world and as an adult I have travelled much of it. In every city and country I have ever visited I make tactical decisions before I step out of the door. Time of day, clothing, route: these things must be considered. Often this is done at a subconscious level; at other times advice might be sought or given. There is a constant tension between the desire to look one's best, to be noticed, and the price that will exact. I want to dress for my destination, the person or people I am going to meet or the event I am headed for, but I must also dress for the men I do not know who I will encounter along the way. Anonymity is something I can only imagine, to walk unguarded an impossibility. Certain places, though, are better or worse than others.

When I start in on the young man in Freetown he apologises almost at once. 'My name is Aminatta,' I tell him. 'And the next time you see me you will remember that and you will use it when you greet me.'

'Yes.'

'Yes what?'

'Yes Aminatta.'

'No!'

The youth looks startled.

'Yes, *Aunty* Aminatta.'

'Yes, Aunty Aminatta.'

Sierra Leone is what some anthropologists have called a 'matriarchy posing as a patriarchy.' It is also a gerontocracy, and deference is expected of anyone younger towards anyone older, even if only by a few years. Over lunch I tell my stepmother what has happened and she laughs. 'Oh, it's those little dresses you wear. They think you're younger than you are.' My mother, sitting sideways on her chair like a Victorian lady riding side-saddle, is dressed in robes arranged in swathes around her. I am wearing a cotton shift dress and sandals. Then: 'Anyway the NGOs brought all that here with them.' She waves a hand as she sips her ginger beer. Freetown then was home to hundreds of Western aid workers, newly arrived in the wake of war. There's a tendency to blame unpalatable social behaviour on outsiders—and yes, everything about those young men (the sagging jeans, the backwards-turned baseball caps, the sullen expressions) spoke of an enthusiasm for American rap—but my stepmother is saying something different. She is saying that they were treating me as if I were a Western woman.

On my first visit to Ghana a couple of years later I have a series of similar encounters: In a hotel a young man in baseball clothes murmurs suggestively as I pass by. I stop and I yell at him. His companion, an older man in a business suit, turns and looks at the young man open-mouthed and orders him to apologise. As they walk away he continues to gesture angrily. The porter with my suitcase asks me what the young man said. He shakes his head: 'They send them to America, you see.' A few days earlier I had taken a walk down the beach at another hotel. There were men working on the scaffolding of a building, and one of them called out to me. I stopped and shouted at him: 'Is that how you talk to your mother?' A local friend who I tell later on will smile at this point in my story. 'So they realised you are an African.' On my way back I had to pass the men again and I was a little concerned about how the next encounter might go, but the men were silent.

I won't make a host of claims about the position of women in West African society and nor will I say that a man will never speak or behave insultingly to a woman in a public space. But I will say this: if he does and if she makes it her business to reply, she can expect the crowd to have her back.

WHOSE SPACE? LOOS, QUEUES AND OTHER PLACES

When I was still at college I read in a newspaper of a study purporting to show that when a man and a woman are walking towards each other on the sidewalk, the woman invariably steps aside for the man. I told my flatmate about it, and the next time we went out she announced gleefully: 'You're doing it! You're doing it!' Ever since then, whenever I think about it, I try to hold my ground and have often found myself nose-to-nose with men who are evidently so used to the path clearing ahead of them they can't figure out where I have come from. In the last year or so the discussion has resurfaced and now the behaviour being described has its own portmanteau, 'manslamming.'

In July of 2017 *New York Times* reporter Greg Howard, a black man, accused white women of doing exactly the same, writing: 'When white women are in my path, they almost always continue straight, forcing me to one side without changing their course. This happens several times a day; and a couple of times a week, white women force me off the sidewalk completely.'

Earlier in the same year I was standing in line for the ladies' in a theatre in Baltimore. The theatre was under renovation, some of the facilities were closed and the line was about fifty people long. Women were making way for very old women and women with disabilities, allowing them to jump the queue. The crowd that night was mostly white and by chance I found myself standing next to the only other woman of colour in the line. A white woman, older (but not so old she might have skipped the queue) and evidently wealthy, walked down the line, stopped halfway and inserted herself just in front of me. I looked at her. I looked around. I caught the eye of the African American woman next to me. 'Did that just happen?' I asked. She raised her eyebrows: 'Don't say anything,' she mouthed. But I did, I said: 'Do you just do that then? Stand wherever in the line you want?' and eventually the white woman slipped out of the line and walked to the back. I asked the African American woman: 'Was it just a coincidence that she stood in front of *us*?' And she replied: 'I'm saying nothing,' and gave me a look like I had been born yesterday.

I return to Helen Moffett, who pointed to how, during apartheid in South Africa, the dominant group, whites, had used methods to regulate blacks in public spaces in ways which reminded them of their subordinate status. It's all about power, people endeavouring, consciously and subconsciously and through myriad daily encounters, to establish dominance over those they consider less worthy. During the Jim Crow era in the United States, white Americans forced upon African Americans the same ignominies as white South Africans did upon their black populations, reserving certain public spaces and privileges for whites. When black people challenged this orthodoxy, it's no coincidence they did it, just as black South Africans did, by walking, by marching, by crossing into those spaces barred to them.

Greg Howard asked an Asian friend, a man, whether he was forced off the sidewalk by white women on the streets of New York. The answer was no. It was the white men who ploughed through him.

Many months ago at a friend's book launch I was standing talking to a man I always liked to talk to whenever we met. He was tall, six foot two or three, and still broad shouldered though he was then in his eighties. We were standing close to the bar, and I was telling a story and turned at one point to find his face suffused with rage. I wondered what could possibly have happened, and I asked him if he was all right. 'He would never, ever have done that thirty years ago,' he eventually said in a low voice. A man on his way to the bar had shouldered him. 'As if I wasn't there.' He'd been manslammed.

I am as certain as I can possibly be that this man had never cat-called a woman, probably was even the kind of person who stepped aside for other people on the sidewalk. By the same token I am equally certain he has never endured a carload of women hurling obscenities at him, heard a woman hiss filth into his ear as he waited to cross a road, or seen a woman waggle her tongue and clutch at her crotch. I remember his face, the mix of fury and frustration, how taken aback I was that he could be so angry, because worse happened to me on any given day.

As I write this I wonder about all those guys, of every class and colour, who have interrupted my thoughts in order to remind me of my place. For whom it was fun to try to unnerve or to humiliate me. To them I say, Just wait. It's coming. Too late for me. Too late for you to learn much except a mote of what it might be like to be treated as if you don't matter. But it's coming.

I'd like to say I wish I were a better person than to feel that way. I wish I could. But I can't.

JULIA ALVAREZ has written novels (*How the García Girls Lost Their Accents, In the Time of the Butterflies, Saving the World, In the Name of Salomé, and ¡Yo!*), collections of poems (*Homecoming, The Other Side/ El Otro Lado,* and *The Woman I Kept to Myself*), nonfiction (*Something to Declare, Once Upon a Quinceañera: Coming of Age in the USA,* and *A Wedding in Haiti*), and numerous books for young readers (including the *Tía Lola Stories* series, *Before We Were Free, finding miracles, Return to Sender,* and *Where Do They Go?*). A recipient of a 2013 National Medal of Arts, Alvarez is one of the founders of Border of Lights, a movement to promote peace and collaboration between Haiti and the Dominican Republic. She lives in Vermont.

A Note on "Penelope" and "Rereading the Classics"

JULIA ALVAREZ

A call came from my agent, Stuart Bernstein, that John Freeman was doing an issue of his anthology, based on the theme of "Taking Back Power." All the contributors would be women. (The theme has since changed to "Power," and the contributors are not limited to women.) Did I have anything to submit?

At that moment I was working on a novel I didn't want to put aside. As part of my research, I had been rereading old journals and memorabilia from the past. We were also moving houses, and the idea was to downsize. Among the yellowed folders, I found one labeled "juvenilia," the term used for fledgling work, before—to quote Dani Shapiro—"the story has become a story." As someone trained solely in the traditional canon, works mostly by white male writers, I had thought that in order for me to be a writer in English, my voice had to be in the register of "Turning and turning in the widening gyre," or "Sing in me, Muse, and through me tell the story," or "Of man's first disobedience, and the fruit . . ." But I couldn't pull it off, that grand music drowned me out. I began listening for subtler strains in what I was reading. These two poems were written in those early years when I was trying to find some semblance of myself in the male text.

Both of these poems offer a perspective toward male power on the page and, as with those height charts we mark on walls, they allow me to review how much (if at all) we've grown in the last forty years. What's disheartening is how much has not changed. I hope that if I revisit them a few years hence, they will not be prescient of that present moment, but instead be tentative, outdated references to a time gone by, juvenilia to store in the attic or burn in the fireplace, Gretel's crumbs that the birds can eat because we are not going back to the disempowerments of the past.

Penelope

I longed for him so much at first
I made my virtue from that longing.
Nights at my window I imagined him
connecting the same stars
into the face of his son, Telemachus,
our bed, his dog, his little loves.
Monthly, the stain upon my sheets
seemed an omen—and I could not sleep
imagining his blood staining the foreign dust.
Thus began my insomniac weaving of cloth.

Others came and camped in our fields—
a moat of suitors—I would laugh,
thinking how little tempted I was.
Some good came of it—my boy,
befriended by would-be fathers,
learned how to dress his arrows, ride
his horse while throwing his spear, touch
a girl so she would want his love, burn
the appropriate sacrifice to the gods.
Often the boy came home, a smirk
on his face, having just proved himself
his father's son, and I would yearn again.

But after some years I will admit I loved
the solitude his absence brought
more than the roughness of his cheek,
his long legs twining mine in sleep. Long nights
before my loom I sang some made-up song
and wove my threads into new shapes
he would have teased were odd.
"What are you making, a winding sheet?"
My life would be his to command again.

He's back, disguised as an old man
to test my virtue, overtake the hall of men
after some drunken bout. Below, in the yard
he stoops to pet the dog, his gestures
recalling that tearful morning he rose
to dress in his battle clothes, and I wept,
my body limp with our lovemaking,
sure that my heart would break.

Now as I watch the old man in the yard
running his eyes over what is his,
I wish he were only his disguise,
a sack of rags, crouched in my yard,
waiting for someone's kind regard.
I wish I could call down to the serving girls
to feed him from the lamb Telemachus
sacrificed to the gods for his father's safety.
Give him some wine in the water bowl
we use for sprinkling the unpacked dust.
I would be rid of him or at least delay
his homecoming for another time.
It frightens me that I who will become
the model of the unwavering loyal wife
should want instead a girl's prerogative—
a life on hold and all night long to weave
a future that my own hands can undo.

Rereading the Classics

We've survived the boys' books and now write our own.
But recently I've been rereading them
listening for my voice in the heavy tomes
that sealed our lips and blocked our lives with plots
we didn't choose ourselves. I've wanted to find
the girl I could have been among the boys,
drawing them drinks of water from a well,
luring them with my song toward the rocks,
handing them mystic apples from a tree:
some semblance of myself in the male text.

Sometimes I find her telling the sultan tales
or telling her father off or sneaking in
to the master bed to be found by Freudian bears.
Most often I'm not there in the pretty girls,
the widowed wives, the mothers nursing sons.
But briefly in the face of the young man
about to set forth on a mythic quest
we'll be reading about for centuries
I'll see a look I'm coming to understand,
the wide world opening like a woman's arms.

NIMMI GOWRINATHAN is a professor and the founder of the Politics of Sexual Violence Initiative at the City College of New York. Her research and writing examine the impact of sexual violence on women's politics, particularly among female fighters; and through the Beyond Identity fellowship program in Harlem, she works closely with young women of color to help them establish their own political projects.

Captive

NIMMI GOWRINATHAN

Nimmi was held captive once—by a Western man, named Dangerous Dan.

Earlier this year, I was in New York City at a panel of worldly writers discussing women in wars. A thoughtful Nigerian author spoke of the #Chibokgirls abducted into extremism. "What of those who chose to stay with Boko Haram?" I asked. A definitive nod before he responded: "That must be the Stockholm syndrome."

Last year, I was in Mexico City to explore the distance between femicide and female vigilantes. Outside the theater, I sat with Ofelia Medina. Medina was an actor before she was a rebel, a rebel before she was an activist. "What of the women who actually join the infamous narcos?" I asked. She shrugged: "This is, you know, the Stockholm syndrome."

The female fighter is this, and that. She is the syndrome; the syndrome is her.

Several years ago, I was in Uppsala, seventy kilometers outside Stockholm, to discuss my work with female fighters. I was taken by the quaintness of the town. Cobblestones invoked an unexpected nostalgia for a time I knew nothing of. There was a strange sense of comfort in those smooth and simple stones.

On the university campus that once hosted the Peace Prize founder Alfred Nobel, before a group of students that included former rebel combatants, I presented my research. The lecture was on my work with women in Sri Lanka's violent separatist movement, the Liberation Tigers of Tamil Eelam (LTTE or the Tigers). Scholars of conflict focus too much, I think, on how the female fighter joins a violent movement (was she a "forced" or "voluntary" recruit?), ignoring why she stays on the battlefield.

It is in fact a lifetime of oppressive moments—the dark molecular makeup of her politics—that matters. Why does an abducted fighter become a high-ranking captain when given the choice to leave? In order to understand her, researchers should adjust their gaze to scan the entire time line of her humanity.

The first question was expected and tiring. "Are you arguing, then, that violence is empowering for women?" No, I am not. You created that word—"empowerment"—to mean the transfer of power from you to her. Also, having been made threadbare through overuse, the word is meaningless.

The second question was unexpected.

A young graduate student, genetically gifted with the type of blinding blond hair Iranians I grew up with in Los Angeles paid good money to replicate, raised his hand. "It seems to me," he said with a certain smugness, "that your theories could all be challenged by the fact that these fighters are simply experiencing the Stockholm syndrome."

A few of his colleagues nodded in relief. The answer was simple.

THE BEGINNING

> *Stockholm syndrome turns victims into victims a second time, by taking from them the power to interpret their own story—and by turning the most significant experiences from their story into the product of a syndrome.*
>
> —Natascha Kampusch

Natascha Kampusch was abducted at the age of ten in Austria and was one of the first women outside Sweden whose stories were diagnosed as an example of the Stockholm syndrome. The viral vernacular had traveled across Europe from Norrmalmstorg Square in Stockholm, where in 1973, three women and one man were taken hostage inside a bank vault.

Outside the bank, inside police lines, was psychiatrist Nils Bejerot, known for his work advocating zero tolerance drug laws (a.k.a. mass incarceration). His brand of behavioral analysis found fault with individuals for the society that failed them. As a criminologist, he positioned himself as a key negotiator between the Norrmalmstorg robbers and the state.

The women inside the vault refused to comply with the demands of the police. They wanted their captors' safety guaranteed. One captive, Kristin Enmark, even maintained a relationship with one of the robbers many years later.

Interviewing the women as the standoff dissipated, Bejerot determined that such strangely un-submissive behavior could be explained only by a syndrome. The method of his diagnosis was questionable, never scientifically validated, and built on a theory that was, essentially, an early incarnation of victim blaming. Yet the Stockholm syndrome constructed a medicalized frame that distorted our view of captive women everywhere.

With ambiguous unsubstantiated "signs" (positive feelings toward the abuser, negative feelings toward authority), the syndrome relied on Bejerot's early theory of "a victim's emotional 'bonding' with the abuser". The syndrome became what critical psychiatrists would call a "received truth" in the medical community—an easy explanation for complex cases.

It would go on to defend Patty Hearst's participation in the Symbionese Liberation Army in California, explain Elizabeth Smart's silence while she was held captive in Utah, limit the lives of prostitutes and

79

battered wives in India, and, eventually, dismiss the politics of female fighters in Sri Lanka.

If you say these girls or me have this syndrome, you don't have to pay attention to what they say.
                                                    —Kristin Enmark

When I began my research, almost twenty years ago now, my advisers pushed me to find the science in political questions, to locate answers that might outlive my activism.

I returned to Sri Lanka that summer determined to do so. As with most budding researchers my early questions were too broad to capture nuance and elicited answers that were too narrow to offer any. "Why did you join the movement?" I asked each former fighter in the contested territory of Batticaloa, in Eastern Sri Lanka. In the beginning, I was fascinated by the feminist grip of pink nails on an AK-47. I was looking for liberation.

Every woman in the Tigers gave me a quizzical look before answering: "I was abducted" or "I had no choice." The women's answers were precise and pointed, and fit within the thin lines of my project.

This was after peace was declared and before the war started again: a brief interlude for reflection. In those days, we would discuss my parents, their childhoods, my siblings, their favorite moments on the battlefield, my marriage prospects, the friends they lost in the jungle, my job, the high-ranking positions they had eventually won.

Despite the intense connections forming between us, I would walk back to my hostel along the edges of the lagoon, in the stillness of the late afternoon heat, disappointed. If these women had no choice from the beginning, surely, they had no power.

But when exactly did choice end and coercion begin?

Just a few months out of the movement, most of the young women had been placed in a vocational training center half a mile from the sparsely furnished rooms where I slept. Church bells, and meticulously presented tea at my doorstep, woke me every morning before I began my walk. I was pulled forward by the life histories of these women I was slowly cataloging across the library table. As I walked I concentrated on my feet, stepping quickly around stray dogs. Whenever I looked ahead, my vision blurred in the pulsating heat.

It was on this walk, on one unremarkable day, that I realized I couldn't see the woman I intended to study: the female fighter. I had enforced my own analytical blackout. The moment of her abduction was the switch to a power outage. Focusing only on her captivity I could not see her power, or her politics.

Prema was one of the fighters who came to chat with me most often. When she met recruiters from the movement in her school classroom, she knew she didn't really have a choice.

"In the beginning, before I joined, I only knew that they [soldiers] had been everywhere, my whole life." Along with several of her classmates she reported for "voluntary" participation at the nearest Tiger camp, where she learned of independence struggles abroad and atrocities against Tamils at home.

She intended to be one of the women her senior commander, Thamilini, spoke of. In her unpublished memoirs, Thamilini writes: "We women of [Tamil] Eelam would one day write stories of courage like the women who joined the battle in the Chinese Red Army, in Palestine, and in Telangana."

Her childhood friend wasn't surprised that she joined the movement. "Since she was a child, Prema has always been very strong-minded—even the boys in school are afraid of her."

"Soon after I joined," Prema told me, "I felt that I had the power to save the Tamils."

everal years later, in a sprawling mansion in Italy owned by the Rockefellers, my summer task was to draw these women's life histories together in some semblance of scholarly order. That was the summer I met Valeria Luiselli. As our friendship deepened over the years, I playfully lobbied for a namesake character to appear somewhere in the pages of her heady handspun fiction.

In the very beginning of Valeria's story of a Mexican family's time in a Southwestern reenactment company, "Shakespeare, New Mexico", we meet Nimmi, "the beautiful, captive Apache girl who lived as a kind of slave with Dangerous Dan". Before it was published, I read through the scenes-within-scenes and found myself rushing to the end.

I was unconcerned with the conditions of Nimmi's captivity: I needed her to be free.

In the Western world every feminist conversation I have been a part of centers on power, and empowerment. A modernized, revamped "royal we" are called upon to give power to the third world woman, birthed into powerlessness. It is a matter of morality, not politics. An imperative meant to be obeyed and never, ever, questioned.

Charity buzz phrases like "community-driven initiatives" and "centering women's voices" cannot change the fact that "we" are the "us" versus "them". Their voices are meant to be uplifted and carefully placed into a dialogue, scripted by us, in the West. Giant placards are held up by unarmed white feminists to prevent the erasure of other women's experiences. Hashtagged helping hands offer choices for women's livelihoods, while hidden small arms sales destroy the opportunity for women to live freely.

When a selective morality overshadows a moment of import—the donning of a hijab; the marriage of an underage girl; the sale of sex; the forced recruitment of a female fighter—the very women we seek to see are disappeared: sometimes, quite simply, through a lazy lexicon.

From that moment forward, a captive woman's thoughts, actions, and calculated inactions are static white noise behind the black bars of her captivity. Through any number of attempts to theorize the oppressed, even the clearest articulation of politics can be heard only as the delusions of a sick, syndrome-struck woman.

Prema had just turned sixteen when she began military training in the Tigers. Sixteen, for Prema, was the beginning, not the end.

THE MIDDLE

If it is a young and vigorous perpetrator, and the victim is a young and romantic woman, a love affair between the parties easily develops. This intensive emotional imprinting may certainly be so strong that it keeps its hold for years afterward; in principle, it may last for life.

—Nils Bejerot

In Luiselli's story, we never find out when or how Nimmi entered into slave-like servitude under Dangerous Dan. We know that she didn't love him, he wasn't a kind man, and she was never entirely subservient. The beginning could have told us more about her life in the middle, but the girl in the middle tells us a lot, tells us more than the woman at the end.

In my first reading, I was drawn to the Nimmi at the end. She was a Nimmi I could never be. It was only much later that I reread the middle. In the middle, Nimmi makes a friend she doesn't need to call an ally: Juana Baca, a Mexican woman who devises a plan for both to escape.

It is here, in captivity, that Nimmi begins to despise Dangerous Dan. She sips milky coffee with Juana, grinds acacia seeds, and dabbles in daydreams of violence.

*Yes, I was afraid of the police; what is so strange about
that? Is it strange that one is afraid of those who are all
around, in parks, on roofs, behind corners, [with] armored
vests, helmets, and weapons, ready to shoot?*
—Kristin Enmark

"I was only in jail once," Janice, a young black woman in Atlanta, tells me with a note of pride. I meet her in the years after Trayvon Martin is killed, and just before Donald Trump takes office.

On the inside there are three girls in a cell, depending on behavior. When the handcuffs capture her as an accessory, she is innocent. Of the many concentric circles that capture her, the largest in diameter and reach is the state. It can touch her, yet she never gets to hold it accountable.

The daily surveilled journey Janice takes to get someplace where she can sleep is familiar. On the short walk from her home to her Atlanta high school, she passes three official police checkpoints. This doesn't include the points where the police just stand, unofficially, to check you.

In jail, and in school, before she picks up a cafeteria tray, there is a metal detector and a pat down.

"We were divided up by behavior; we were all black but, you know, the bad ones were known to be more 'thuggish'." Here in the safe space of activists at Project South, she rarely smiles. In there, she smiles to survive. In the presence of her captors, to "act crazy" would extend the length, and brutality, of her captivity.

In her skin, in this community, incarceration is a birthright.

At a nail salon in midtown Manhattan, Fathima tells me, "Being born into my community, you are born into bondage." In India, where she has just come from, her nomadic community is associated by caste with trading cattle.

Earlier that day we had been eating vegetarian Indian food amid white business lunchers. In the restaurant she shifted uneasily, looking up only to offer hardened one-word answers to questions I quickly stopped asking. I suggested we get a manicure. In Sri Lanka, the girls and I often spoke most easily over nail polish fumes. We would carefully paint and repaint our nails—all of us offering tidbits of ourselves while admiring our handiwork.

Fathima is pleased with the large sequins embedded in the gold paint she chooses. She is comfortable enough now to express her discomfort in an examination chair that follows her everywhere. "Sometimes I just don't want to talk about my husband. I hate him." A male salon staffer starts to massage her shoulders and she jumps, pushing him away. Everyone in America is too close for comfort, and too far away for solace.

On the subcontinent marriage is inevitable. To whom and when are choices presumed to be predetermined: by God, the Party, and the State. Or, in contemporary India, the three heads of one omnipotent overseer.

When her parents tied the cotton thread around her hands, binding her in marriage to her husband, they knew he was a pimp. Fathima was nine years old then. "My parents, they thought they are making the right choice, by sending me out of Nepal." Between a life of herding animals in the mountains, and one caged in an urban slum as a prostitute, her parents made a choice.

Now that she is free, she is in New York to raise funds for victims of trafficking still in captivity. Whether for tsunami victims or child brides, fund-raisers always seem to me like a necessary evil. A performance for the powerful.

On this occasion she surveys the catered spread from the top of Tribeca, nearly eye-level with the lofty tip of the Freedom Tower. She finds the buffet choices distasteful, and whispers softly, "Everything looks uncooked. So far in America, I only like the Mexican fried shrimp." She serves herself a few grapes and a piece of cheese. The austere gaping space, adorned with a few select prints notable for their rarity, has an air of isolation meant to be envied. One that penetrates her in the most unenviable way.

She stands off to the side as the guests gather. A nouveau riche, cultured, socially conscious crowd—people for whom an invitation to such events is an increasingly necessary symbol of status. The type of crowd that admires both the Fendi Casa coffee table and the copy of "Guerrilla Warfare" conspicuously lying on it.

They come bearing their power, ready for the one transaction (via tax-deductible gift) they are happy to conduct themselves. They will defer to her pain, and demand inspiration from it.

She is wearing a salwar kameez with sparkling red and green bhandara work, partially covered by an oversize charcoal blazer—a nod to the business side of it all. She is pleased with the gray high-top sneakers she bought in Times Square. The large beads on her costume jewelry suggest she has drawn from the accessories she has reserved for special occasions.

Fathima shares handpicked details of her disempowered life with the crowd that encircles her. Married as a child, she was held captive; she was beaten; she watched, every day, as girls were sold to her husband.

The audience is drawn close enough into the intimacy of Fathima's wounds to feel an easy sympathy but positions itself far enough away to escape a more demanding empathy. This is a moment I have seen before—where heart and purse strings become entangled. One opens to release the other from responsibility.

There is a silence, a collective chest tightening, as the audience waits for the empowering ending it can celebrate.

When she is free.

"But him, he is there, a celebrity. He is free," Shivanee says. The abuser is revealed here, in this inner circle. I am sitting among activists in Canada; there is love and respect—for experiences, pronouns, and colonized lands. We are all still settling into the strange territory of a conversation genuinely guided by a collective desire to center the victim of sexual violence, and her experience.

"You know who he is, you see his face on the billboards," Shivanee says. The Tamil, Sri Lankan, island version of an African "big man". In oversize advertisements and cultural life the community holds him up. Waiting in the wings, she reminds us, are "uncles-in-training".

In an expansive community of Toronto Tamils, social circles are small and overlapping. The triangular space where they meet is sharply defined by a collective silence.

It is a silence we have become accustomed to in its overshadowing oppression, and its constant presence in the Tamil language, a placeholder for violence. We had, all of us, heard these words before:

"Ah, yes, she couldn't marry because, *that*, you know . . ."

"She was fine until . . . *this* . . . happened."

Rape is this, and that.

There is, in fact, a word for it in Tamil, Shivanee reminds us: "katpazhi". She repeats it. Broken into its composite parts, it means: "katpu" (chastity) and "azhi" (destroy). "Azhi" can also mean erase.

"I don't think I've ever used the word, though. When I get angry with a Tamil man, I get so angry I switch to English," Shivanee says. The language of the incident is less relevant than the reporting of it. "If you say anything, you get pushed outside the community, outside the circle."

A longtime activist against sexual violence defines the circular lines she lives by. "I follow the three-six-nine rule. I can only directly support the woman three feet from me. I can only hope that she impacts the family six feet from me, and the community nine feet from me." In this configuration, she manages expectations of social change, acknowledging the levers of state power that are out of her reach.

Shivanee prefaces what she says about her abuser with the language of the Stockholm syndrome, a caveat that compromises her own clarity. "Maybe this is just the victim's complex talking, but we should think about the pressures of Tamil masculinity, the problem of the perpetrator." The Diagnostic and Statistical Manual of Mental Disorders rejects its legitimacy every year, and yet the syndrome can speak through her.

These activists yearn for action, even as they crave the space for premeditation. Justice should be active—a swinging gavel. Someone swings, someone else is smashed. Action yields immediate rewards, the emotive sustenance to continue. And yet, to someone sitting in the middle of generationally violated women, justice seems permanently delayed.

"It doesn't matter, anyway," Shivanee sighs. "You don't have time for justice when you're working class, when you have a two-hour commute in Toronto in the winter."

Some suggest moving backward to move forward—remembering grandmothers who fashioned palmyra leaves into patterned baskets, sat in circles where marital abuse stories were woven into the laughter of commiseration. They didn't leave their men, but they did line the insides of lipstick cases with the numbers of domestic violence hotlines.

"We have no illusions that society was built for us," Shivanee says. For them as immigrants, Tamils, and women, dependency is a cultural legacy. "Even within that, trying to survive . . . is exhausting."

Creating a cocoon of normality within the framework of a crime is not a syndrome.

—Natascha Kampusch

THE END

Significantly, the women in the bank drama did not have to act violently to be medicalized; it was the fact that they acted at all that was taken as a pretext for regarding them as sufferers of a psychiatric condition.

—Cecilia Åse, Professor, Stockholm University

With the exception of the occasional male Nazi sympathizer, the Stockholm syndrome has always been used to explain behavior of women that men find surprising. A Swedish police officer, who later questioned Dr. Bejerot's methods, concedes, "The Stockholm syndrome is a gender thing, actually. It is quite easy to silence a woman just by saying these things."

If, in the beginning, there was force or coercion, the syndrome predicts the outcome in the end. The middle is skipped over, dismissed, medicalized away. But the movement is in the middle, where women are navigating within the circumstances they were given and those they create. In Sweden, Mexico, and New York City I heard the same diagnosis. From marginalized American, Indian, and Tamil–Sri Lankan women, I heard the same lines of resistance. For women held captive, sentiments and politics intersect to form a matrix for nonlinear transformation—from the inside, out.

O*n marriage:* "The hardest part, for me, is feeling stuck inside the mind-set of other people." As she nears eighteen, marriage looms ahead. She isn't looking forward to it. The weight of a heavily embroidered veil will cover her head, the one place on her body without any wounds. In order to leave, she needs a plan. She begins by asking her husband for a favor. She waits until his head is wobbly, his arms are too limp to hit her. Together, the wives leave the house in search of oil. When they are denied, shamed because of who they are, the women beat the policemen over the head with plastic tumblers. They get the oil.

and . . .

Community: "I do want to be free. But for us, the cage is on the inside. It was my destiny to be captured." The unarmed men are the more immediate threat. She smiles, a grim smile, recalling a recent incident. One man, in particular, would come home drunk and beat his wife. It was a small enough community that even secret abuses were conducted out loud.

One day, he was stopped, just before reaching home. Several wives were waiting, rope in hand. Together, they tied him to a tree in a prominent community space. He promptly passed out.

and . . .

State violence: "On the outside, people will still see you as a 'nigger'—it feels like you can't do anything about that." There had always been violence outside her home. Men in militias. This violence was called political. Group loyalties shifted with the ease of money changing hands. Trust built only through funds eventually collapsed community ties.

An agent for securing the Homeland tells me, "People keep worrying about the police becoming militarized. Really, in America, the military should be trained by the police. They are much more sophisticated in both surveillance and capture."

and . . .

Resistance: "I became a very good fighter, on the outside. In the end, I still would not have left. Because I was taken at eighteen, now someone else will make the choice for me."

In the end, Nimmi ties a drunkenly obedient Dangerous Dan to a hitching post. She slaps him a couple of times. She places a heavy stone on top of his head. When he lets it fall, she slaps him again— and puts the stone back on his head.

EPILOGUE

In 2009, heavily armed by an unholy alliance of religious states, a humanitarian operation wiped out the Tigers in Sri Lanka, and nearly one hundred thousand civilians. It was the marketed happy ending to decades of war (promises of ever after were not included). Last year, a senior military commander tells me, speaking of the former female fighters with pride, "We saved these Tamil women. Look, see, we have made them beautiful, we have made them women again."

Prema won't meet me until it's dark. Against the pull of thirty-something hormones, she is much thinner than she was when we first met, when she was in her mid-twenties. Cell phones light the pathway through damaged homes to a tiny patio. Her own cell phone, a gift from the army, sits at the bottom of a well.

"That is what they use," she says, "to track you." Calls from the soldiers are more frequent at night. We stand in the glow of the next-door neighbor's kitchen lamp. Children and older aunties huddle on the porch, fixated on our shadowy outlines, the only possible form of evening entertainment.

She was captured in the final days of fighting. Months in detention bled into months of de-radicalization. Before the army would believe she had been defused as a threat, she had to learn to sew. Now, she has two choices: to work in a beauty salon or push a pastry cart, with her one good leg.

Nearly a decade earlier, she had told me, "I wasn't sure I wanted to join. But what they told us, in the movement, is still true. Tamils, in this state, we are slaves. Who doesn't want to live free, not as slaves?"

Days before she meets me again, a government soldier brags of their surveillance, "If there's a wedding, a gathering, we know that it's happening." He smiles, "We know what Tamils eat for lunch."

They hold her picture, track her movements, register her activities. Every checkpoint has a cashier's notebook filled with the details of her life. She knows of others, fighters, whose fear pushed them to exchange sex for security.

Everything goes suddenly dark. Prema sharply commands one of the children to bring the kerosene lamp, used sparingly to avoid begging for oil from the military. She strikes the match just in front of her face. Before she lights the wick, she looks at me. "I am very angry, all the time. If I could, I would join again."

> *There was no one in the main square except for Dangerous Dan—still tied to the hitching post—so deeply asleep that he appeared dead, his head drooping. Nimmi was standing guard beside him, holding a shotgun. She fired twice into the wide, open sky.*
>
> —Valeria Luiselli

The Cottage

LAN SAMANTHA CHANG

Another man had wanted Chun. A heavyset accountant, he took them out for barbecue and drove a silver car. But after two meetings, they found out that he kept a woman and a daughter in a city not far away.

Taichuang and Chun had known each other as children. Over a lunch Chun and her aunt had made together at home, Taichuang told them that he would soon finish his degree and take a job at a school in California. A librarian's salary was small, but enough for a beginning.

Chun tried and failed to imagine him working in rows of faded books. He had been a fleet runner as a child and now his torso tapered to his waist in a clean line. He smelled of soap. After lunch, they escaped her aunt's apartment. They walked past their old school, peering in at the children tucked over their desks. Chun lingered on the playground, idling on a swing. She felt his hands take the swing from behind. "Hang on," he said, and pulled her back and up; then he was holding her at a pleasurably ambitious height, the world all blue and brightly silent. He released the swing. She tipped back into the sudden fall, savoring the rush out to the point where gravity jerked her down, then swooped back to him waiting. She thought, It could be, it might be like this—

"You could do worse," said her aunt when he had gone. They had no money themselves. And while Chun considered the resigned pettiness of this remark, and beneath the pettiness, the sense of something precious being discarded, her aunt pushed out her bottom lip and said, "How pretty do you think you are?"

They married in 1990 and Chun flew to America. They lived in a town not far from Taichuang's university, where they rented a blue-shuttered house with a mossy, tiled roof—really a cottage—on a silent, sunlit street, one of a row that had been built when the acreage was a peach orchard. Through the thin walls baked a solid, airless heat. It was not the kind of house to own, he said. It would not be sheltering for a child, he said, when they could afford to have a child. His statements freed her from the cottage and she did not mind it. They had their names on the mailbox and a listing in the telephone book. She was sorry about his American name, T.C.—she would have preferred that he had chosen the name Charlie—but he said, "Why choose a name that you and I cannot pronounce?"

"Then Jack," she said, "Why not Jack?"

"I am nothing like a Jack," he said. "I am not reckless, like the Jack of Hearts, and I am not rich and powerful like a Kennedy."

He said this in a kind way that made it wrong for her to wish that he were anything else. At least she could choose her own name, and she chose Ruby—it was listed in the phone book: "T.C. and Ruby Yang"—yet he still called her Chun.

They grew wax beans on wires strung up along the eastern wall of the cottage. She kept two patches of chives; four sprawling, hairy cucumber plants; four hot peppers; and four tomatoes. She measured out the water and poured it carefully, near the stems, in the morning when the earth was cool. T.C. asked if she would like a rosebush. Chun shrugged, not because she didn't want roses, but because she felt reluctant to acknowledge that the plant would be an extravagance. T.C. earned close to three hundred dollars a week. One seventy-nine was paid each month for the brown Chrysler he drove to work. Every other week, the morning after payday, she rode her bicycle to the bank in the shopping plaza, where she deposited the check in their account.

Rice cost thirty-nine cents in half-pound bags, but a fifty-pound bag could be bought for only a few dollars. The bulk variety was rougher, with hulls and small stones to pick out now and then, so for each meal she measured out the raw rice, poured it into a shallow blue bowl, and searched for stones.

For making chicken with green beans, the backs and necks were cheapest; when they did buy chicken breasts, Chun sliced each breast not once but twice into shreds the size and shape of matchsticks. She topped and tailed the beans so carefully that the little pile of ends contained no flesh. She knew how from watching the aunt who had raised her, in another household where the labor had been cheaper than food. There had been endless folding and rolling of dumpling skins, the bit of filling for each dumpling meanly pinched by chopsticks. Every morsel of precious meat came packaged in its bite of starch. Each day T.C. brought a brown paper bag to work containing an apple and fried rice, or, as a treat, a sandwich for which she counted two slices of ham, tucking in the edges.

That the deed to a house could be purchased with a down payment —scrabbled together of pennies and dimes collected after the garden was tended and the chicken was sliced into matchsticks—seemed, to Chun, like a magic trick. She knew this wasn't so, and yet it seemed that such a thing required procedures of magic, and so she pursued her routines as if they were rituals and kept her wishes unspoken. She lay awake at night, adding sums, her calculations comforting her against a fear that hovered when they turned out the lights. At the start of his third year, T.C. received a raise of twenty-three dollars per week—eight percent, a lucky number. It was Chun's idea to live the way they had always lived, to put the extra money into the bank while waiting for the house. Although she knew their money was not physically in a vault, she tried to imagine it there, a pile of bills in a drawer, behind the big chrome door, round and intricate as a watch.

After four years, they had saved enough for a down payment. And yet there were uncertainties. The market was on the rise, the broker told T.C. This meant, she knew, that their money was now worth less; that night, in the dark, Chun imagined the pile of bills measlier, smaller. "It's a matter of numbers," T.C. pointed out. "It doesn't mean we worked any less hard or saved any less. It simply means we should buy soon, and that we have to buy what we can afford, or we'll be priced out of the market."

In her next letter to her aunt, Chun tried to describe her hovering fear. "I've never felt this way," she wrote. "You've never had money before," her aunt wrote back. "If you think you're frightened now, just wait until you have a child." And yet this was not exactly the problem, Chun thought in the night. The problem was that she might try and try, scrimp and save as well as she possibly could, but it would not be enough. And then, as if her fear were a dark suitor and she its bride, she felt its shape near the bed.

They looked at many houses, but eventually, at two. The gray house, they were told, was what they could afford. And yet their explorations led them over and over to the yellow house. It was not simply that *she* liked it more; she knew T.C. liked it better as well.

He pointed out the virtues of the gray house. "It has an extra bedroom," he said. A bedroom for a child or even two children. Plus it had small windows, he said. Houses with small windows cost less to heat, and they were cool in the summer. The house had been built after the war, when every nail and every scoop of Spackle was precious. It had been built with the idea that someday its inhabitants might want to finish things off themselves—to finish building the fireplace and chimney, to turn the attic into living space. Except none of them, in fifty years, had done this—their circumstances had forced them to live with what they had.

"Why—" she began.

"What is it?"

Why must a small house be so very mean? Why must the kitchen be so dark, the cabinets cramped, the window a simple cutout in the wall, plain and unadorned like the lidless eye of a spinster? Why did the front door open over such a narrow sill into the small front room? The real estate agent said the house was a "starter," and Chun took a momentary comfort from the word, as if it would be no time at all before the possession of the house lay in their past. But first it would be theirs. For an indeterminate number of years, their house, and their lives shaped within it. She had begun to see that it was not easy to be rid of things. An existence in a place, once one had come to live it, took on a weight that, while not the yoke of permanence, could not be lightly discarded. One could not get rid of the brown Chrysler if there was nothing wrong with it; it could not be jettisoned for lack of distinction. One could not get rid of a marriage. One could not ignore the passage of the years.

"Tell me what you want," he said.

It was the world's ruthlessness she feared, its shining cruelty.

She reached for it.

"I want the yellow house," she said.

"All right," he said. "Let's see if we can afford it."

Again they went over the numbers: the amount they had in the bank, the amount their best loan was now worth, the amount they needed for the yellow house and its repairs. But they could not buy the house. Merely to repaint would cost them several thousand, and paint would wear away—a dozen years or so would finish it—dry, brittle, and uneven in the relentless sun of central California. Over time, the money would add up. Money always added up: small sums became large sums over time; this went for expenditures as well as savings.

"You haven't felt misfortune," her aunt told her the next day, her birthday. Their phone conversations took place three times a year: their birthdays, and the lunar new year. "Someday," she said, "when you are older and come to see the world like everybody else, you will come to understand that what you are living now is deep, unchallenged happiness."

They went out to dinner to celebrate her birthday. It was T.C.'s idea, an extravagance, but they were about to buy a house, he said. Chun had been curious about the restaurant for some time. She admired its pretty crimson awning and Italian name. But she felt the price and the worth and the lost opportunity in every bite.

"Are you sorry," he said, after she placed her order, "that you did not marry that other man?"

"Of course not," she said, reflexively. The accountant and his luxuries were now a blurred memory.

That Friday, with T.C.'s paycheck in its envelope tucked into her purse and the purse strapped over her shoulder, Chun rode her bicycle into the west side of the shopping plaza lot. It was a large parking lot with two bicycle racks, one near the grocery store and the other near the bank. Chun went to the rack by the bank.

After making her deposit, she came out of the bank and noticed, parked nearby, a long, low car. It was an older model, a subtle dark blue, every inch of it cleaned and polished.

A woman sat behind the wheel. Later, Chun would tell T.C. she might have been in her forties, although Chun found it hard to tell, for there was not a wrinkle or shadow in her face and yet there seemed to be, in her honeyed skin, a patina of years. There was something elegant but weary in the way she gazed ahead, looking not at the shopping center but beyond it, at the foothills bright in the lushness of recent rains. She regarded Chun for a moment through the rolled-down window, then her eyes moved to the doorway of the bank from which she had come. Now the woman looked back at Chun. Her eyes were notable for their unusually light green, and for their steadiness.

"You wouldn't have a lighter, would you?"

She spoke in a low voice with a deep velvet center, but flinty around the edges. Her pronunciation, admirably precise, had just a hint of a slow and liquid sound in the vowels. She was not from California; and Chun felt a sudden wish to be a person with roots deep in the continent, in a lush place, perhaps, where the leaves of oak trees, rather than crinkling in the heat, spread wide and soft out in the moist air. There was something sure and finished in this woman's way of talking; it was as if, from where she sat in her low car, she could see the shape of everything coming.

Chun wanted to speak to her. "No," she said, meeting the green eyes, "I'm sorry." In the eyes there remained the expression of bright expectancy. Chun had no lighter; she had never taken up smoking when she was younger. But she did have matches. She had slipped them into her purse after the celebration dinner. There had been a china bowl on the counter by the door, heaped with the shiny little boxes.

With a sense of triumph, she opened her purse and found the matches.

The woman held up the matchbox in her long hand, admiring it. "This looks like a nice place," she said.

"Yes," said Chun. Then, venturing further, "It was a celebration."

"It's always good to celebrate," the woman said in a friendly way. "Do you mind my asking what occasion?"

"No, I don't mind," Chun said. "No special occasion." Then, as the woman lit the cigarette in her graceful hands, she took a breath and said in a rush, "We are going to buy a house. And it was my birthday."

"Your birthday," the woman said. She blew a thin stream of smoke, ignoring the mention of the house. "How old are you?"

"Twenty-seven."

"Twenty-seven. You know, where I come from, they say that twenty-seven is a lucky number," she remarked.

"Oh," Chun said. There was something about this stranger that made her wish to venture out into the world. "Do you come from far away?"

"In a way. I'm here now." She reached the matchbox back toward Chun.

"No," Chun said, suddenly. "You can keep it."

"Thank you." To Chun's chagrin, and delight, the woman did not refuse the gift. She looked appraisingly at the box of matches. Then she undid her purse. It was an old-fashioned clutch that opened wide. From where Chun stood, she could see that the purse was filled with paper bills, stacked together and curled and held together with metal clips.

After a moment, the woman followed Chun's gaze. "Yes," she said. "I should keep my purse in neater order."

She slid her hands into the purse and drew out a pile of bills, then began to neaten them as if they were a pile of playing cards. She did not seem to mind sitting in her car with a stranger watching her stack one pile of bills atop another. The stack grew so high that it was difficult to tidy. And the bills were not ones, or even tens— Chun saw hundred-dollar bills sliding carelessly beneath her hands.

"I received some income," she explained. "I was just taking this to the bank."

"How—" Chun struggled to find the words.

"I make investments. My father does it for me, really. They're reasonable, small, and they produce a regular income."

"What kind of investments?" She could not stop watching the money in the woman's hands.

"Oh, this and that. My dad has a finger in a lot of pots, as they say."

Chun thought about this and smiled.

"It's a funny expression, I know," the woman said. "But it describes him to a T. A jack of all trades, we call him. A wheeler-dealer. Some of the investments are in businesses, and sometimes he just gives me advice. His suggestions have a way of making good returns."

With such an income she could do anything. "What are your plans for the money?" Chun asked.

"Plans? I don't really make that many plans," she said. "I do what I want."

The meaning of this came slowly. She and T.C. had plans for every penny; their dreams themselves were tallied in dollars and cents. She thought of the chicken backs and necks, the vegetables watered, and the leftover lunches T.C. took to work as a series of numbers, pennies and dimes, and she thought of the meals prepared as a kind of deposit—a deposit in labor, almost a sacrifice, she was making for the future—which would be worth all of it, somehow, more than worth it, for a future when she would be freed of the present.

But T.C. didn't mind the present. He was happy with the small house, knowing exactly what it was worth and was not worth, and he did not mind that all the world could see what he was worth and not worth. And he was happy with her, with her small dinners and her small charms. He was a good husband, she understood, and after they had moved into the gray house, he would make a good father.

The woman was saying, "I can ask him to show you, if you want. Would you like that?"

"Y-yes," Chun said, cautiously, watching as she piled the money.

"My father and I could come over, one of these evenings, and he could tell you and your husband about it."

"Yes," she said.

"I don't know for certain, but I think he would be willing to bring you in. You look like a good person, a deserving person. And, I'm sure, your man."

"Yes," Chun said. "He is."

"How about next week?" She asked where Chun lived and Chun told her.

"That's settled, then. Of course, you would need something to invest. Some seed money. Something I could show him. Do you think you've got a little to spare?"

Chun considered the question. There was the bank, and the bank account. "How much?"

The woman thought for a moment. "Well, it would have to be enough to make a start," she said. "Probably more than a few thousand."

A few thousand.

"You don't have it?"

"We do," she said. "It's just that"—she felt embarrassed—"I would have to ask my husband."

"Of course," the woman said. "And of course, you wouldn't need to do this at all."

"Yes," Chun said, relieved. "I suppose I needn't do it at all."

The woman closed her purse, shutting the money out of sight. "It was good to talk to you," she said. "What is your name?"

"My name is Ruby."

"It was good to meet you, Ruby. Maybe we'll run into each other here again."

"Yes," Chun said. But when? The woman had set her purse down beside her and was putting her key in the ignition. She was not looking at Chun anymore. Chun put one foot on the bike pedal and looked away, out of the parking lot toward her house, and it seemed to her that the parking lot looked smaller, with fewer cars, and that something small awaited her at the end of it. She heard the low rumble of the engine.

"Good-bye, Ruby. See you around."

"Wait," Chun said.

Patiently, the woman turned off the engine and brought her green eyes back toward Chun.

"How much money would it take," Chun asked, "to really . . . make a start?"

"Oh," the woman tipped her head to one side. "About twenty thousand."

They had twenty-six thousand in their savings account.

In the branch bank, the woman waited nearby while Chun filled out the withdrawal slip. How many times had she filled out the other slip, the opposite way? She handed it to the teller. "I want to make a withdrawal."

She spoke clearly, but the teller waited, glancing at the woman by her side.

"Ma'am, are you sure you want to do this?"

Chun straightened. "Yes."

The teller eyed Chun, then said, "I'll need approval for this. Just a moment." She left the counter and returned with an older man.

"Mrs. Yang," he said. "Are you sure that you would like to make this withdrawal?"

In his expression she saw kindness. But he was a small man, timid even in his kindness.

"Yes."

"Do you want the money in hundreds?"

Chun turned to the woman standing next to her, and found refuge in the confidence of her green eyes.

"Hundreds would be ideal." She examined her hands with care and Chun noticed that except for the one ragged nail, the others looked smooth and polished.

The teller fussed for quite some time counting the money. She went through the bills three times, as if she had nothing else to do but stretch out the minutes. Chun felt a sudden impatience. "That's fine," she said. The teller put the bills in a large envelope and handed it to Chun. "You take care of that, now," she said.

Chun took the envelope and turned away. When they left the bank, the bright sunlight met them; for a moment she could not see.

"I thank you for this," the woman said, and in her voice was sincere warmth.

"You're welcome," Chun said.

"I'll be in touch, Ruby," she said. "I think you'll be glad."

"Yes," Chun said.

Then the woman started the car again and drove away.

Chun went back to her bicycle. The handlebars felt strong and solid in her palms; her legs seemed to have become curiously lightened. The ride home through the hot, floating afternoon felt limitless, yet brief. She began to think of the possibilities ahead. The yellow house, or even a larger, more imposing house, with an entrance that opened onto a yard filled with roses, peonies, snapdragons. She stepped lightly over the threshold to the cottage. In the cool, dark kitchen, she counted out three dried mushrooms to soak for the meal; washed the chicken breast and sliced it once, then twice; then the peppers; then the tofu and button mushrooms. She topped and tailed the wax beans.

She would not bear a child for another five years.

Standing at the sink, while rinsing the raw rice and searching for stones, Chun heard a car pull into the driveway. She raised her hand to her throat.

NICOLE IM is a writer based in New York City. She was born and raised in California and recently completed an MFA in nonfiction at the New School.

On Sharks and Suicide

NICOLE IM

1.

He died after just three days. The eleven-and-a-half-foot great white shark was caught off the coast of Japan and taken to the Okinawa Churaumi Aquarium on January 5, 2016. During his captivity, he refused to eat and smashed his body against the walls. On the third day, he sank to the bottom of the tank and the staff could not revive him.[1] I wonder what it must've been like for that shark, used to the silence and expanse of the ocean, to be imprisoned behind glass, barraged with the incessant chattering of humans and their gawking faces and pointing fingers, the clicking and flashing of their cameras. What other form of escape did he have?

In December of 2016, I spent four days under suicide watch at Metropolitan Hospital in New York City. If I had known that calling the National Suicide Prevention Lifeline meant involuntary admission to the nearest psych ward, I never would have called. Cutting is a walk on a tightrope. One slip and it's all over. Dangerous, I know, but when I slice into my own skin, I am god, and fuck, does having that kind of power feel good. There is a difference between the desire to cut myself and the desire to kill myself. The trouble is they sometimes overlap, crashing into each other like rolling waves.

I called the hotline because in that particular moment, both waves were sweeping me under. It wasn't that I had cut myself too deep and was unable to stop the bleeding. It was that even after making over two dozen cuts along my forearm, I still wanted more. The god inside me was angry, and she demanded I continue the blood sacrifice. The voice on the other end of that hotline became my life preserver, and I grabbed on until I was able to find my breath again.

"Thank you for talking to me," I said. "I think I'm okay now."

I set down the dripping razor blade and stared at the red streaks on my arm outlined in purple bruises.

"I need to send someone to check on you," the voice said.

"I'm not feeling suicidal anymore," I replied.

And it was true. The waters calmed. The blood running down my arm appeased the voice in my head telling me to kill myself. I had bled enough. For now.

"I'd feel better if someone could just check on you," the voice urged. "But don't worry, they won't take you to the hospital."

2.

"We are legally obligated to take you to the hospital," the female EMT said in a monotone voice. Her partner yawned so wide I could see the black fillings in his molars. Two police officers stood further back in the doorway. One was on his phone. The other stared at me with something like disdain, like how dare I waste his time and the taxpayers' money.

"The hotline said you were just going to check on me. I don't want to go anywhere."

Officer One shifted his eyes to Officer Two. I eyed the guns holstered to their hips.

"Well, you did cut yourself," the female EMT said, "and like I just said, we are legally obligated to take you."

110

They all took a step closer, spreading out to form a semicircle around me. I was escorted out of my apartment and into an ambulance, buckled in, and driven to Metropolitan Hospital. Over the next five hours, I was poked and prodded, told to pee in a cup, asked if I heard voices or felt homicidal, had ever taken drugs, or was on drugs right now.

"No, no, no, and no."

At dawn, when I asked again if I could leave, they handed me a one-page document titled "Notice of Status and Rights Emergency Admission."

It basically boils down to this: you have none.

3.

According to an article in *Psychology Today*, sharks do not feel pain. At least, not in the same way humans and other animals do. Nociceptors—receptors that register tissue damage, heat, and pressure—are not present in sharks, and they do not seem to respond to painful stimuli. For example, hammerhead sharks regularly eat stingrays and have been found with as many as ninety-six barbs embedded in their mouths.[2] Treatment for stung humans includes soaking the wound in lidocaine, and even then the pain may still be so extreme that "a regional nerve block may be needed."[3] *Wimpy humans*, the hammerhead must think. Whalers have also reported seeing sharks continue feeding after being bitten or even disemboweled by other sharks.[4]

It seems that on every level sharks were designed to make things bleed. Great whites have up to five rows of developing teeth lining their jaws, and over a lifetime, they will grow and lose close to thirty thousand.[5] What are sharks if not cold-blooded killers? But perhaps they are more complicated than their outward physiology suggests. Is it anthropomorphizing them too much to suggest that sharks have the capacity to feel anger, frustration, distress, despair? The tank in Okinawa was clean, kept at a comfortable temperature, and pumped with the right levels of oxygen. The shark was given plenty of food. So what other reason would he have to sink to the bottom of the tank and refuse to swim, if it wasn't that he had lost his will to live?

4.

"You're here for your own good," the nurse told me. "Come, let me show you where you sleep."

She led me down the hall into one of the bedrooms and pointed to the first bed on the right side of the room. There were four beds in all, each in a corner. There was a tall cabinet between each two beds with doors on the sides instead of on the front. Half a cabinet for each patient. The bathroom was on one side of the room, the shower on the other—doors but no locks. A woman was huddled under a single sheet in the bed in the far left corner. Her bare feet stuck out at the bottom. The hem of her pajama bottoms was dirty and frayed and her heels were dry and cracked. I wondered how long she'd been there.

"You can shower between seven and nine a.m. or between eight and nine thirty p.m.," the nurse said. "It's off-limits outside of those times. You stay here and rest, okay?"

I sat on the end of the bed the nurse said was mine and stared at the sleeping bodies around me. I noticed that above each bed was a handmade poster with the patient's name written in marker and decorated with stickers. JOANIE. DAKOTA. CELESTE. I turned around, relieved to see a blank space. I needed to get out of there before someone decided I needed a name poster, too. This was not where I wanted to belong.

"This is your new home," I imagine a staff member having told the great white as he dumped a bucket of squid into the tank. "You'll learn to like it here."

5.

"Does it hurt?" the nurse asked, handing me what looked like a ketchup packet of Neosporin.

It didn't, and the lack of pain was infuriating. I needed something sharp to cut through the claustrophobic fog of this nightmare. The ward was hot and stuffy, and its pale blue walls made me want to claw out my own eyes. I dug my fingernails into the palms of my hands as hard as I could. Pain surged up my arm. Slight relief.

The nurse watched as I spread ointment on the cuts. Beads of red sprang to the surface. She handed me a tissue.

"Just blot gently."

I didn't want to do anything gently. I wanted to cut. I imagined pushing the tip of a razor deep into my wrist and dragging it up my forearm. I'd watch my skin part on either side of the blade. It would be just like unzipping a jacket. Blood would spill out of me, warm, wet, thick, deep red. The world around me would blur at the edges, then fade away completely. If I couldn't have my blade, I would take what I could get. I wanted to grab the nurse's pen and ram it into my neck. I wanted to run and slam my head against the wall until it split open. I wanted to throw a chair at the window, shatter the glass, and fall nine stories onto the New York City concrete.

I hated being trapped between those walls while doctors, nurses, medical aides, social workers, and deliverymen filtered in and out. I hated them for their freedom.

Once the nurse left the table, one of the other patients, Joanie, came over and sat in the empty chair across from me.

"That's evil," she said, pointing at my arm.

She stared with big brown bloodshot eyes. She had frazzled gray hair that stuck out in every direction, as if she had just stuck her finger into an electrical socket. She was missing several teeth, so that when she spoke, she lisped and her lips seemed to work overtime like a fish in search of food. She looked from side to side as if she were on the lookout for eavesdroppers, then pressed the palms of her hands onto the tabletop and leaned in close to me.

"It's the devil making you do that," she whispered. "Don't listen to him."

I leaned away from her, unsure of how to respond.

Maybe Joanie was right. Maybe it was an evil spirit telling me to cut, and all I had to do was refuse to listen to it. But there were two voices in my head. And if I ignored the voice telling me to cut, I would be overpowered by the voice telling me to kill myself. There was a battle raging inside me, and I was both enemy and ally.

6.

Until the 1930s, self-harm behaviors were regarded by mental health professionals as attempts at suicide. Psychiatrist Karl Menninger was the first to suggest that self-harm behaviors including cutting, burning, and even bone breaking did not stem from suicidal ideation but were coping mechanisms, a way to channel otherwise overwhelming emotional pain into a physical, visible, controllable one.[6] In his 1938 book *Man Against Himself*, Menninger writes that "local self-destruction is a form of partial suicide to avert total suicide."[7] He goes on to say that when self-harm is viewed in this way, "it represents a victory, even though sometimes a costly one, of the life instinct over the death instinct."[8]

Interestingly, though, despite the emotional turmoil that leads to self-harm behaviors, many people report not feeling any physical pain when they injure themselves. In *A Bright Red Scream*, Marilee Strong writes that because many self-injurers harm themselves while in dissociated states, they are not aware of the pain and that "some are not even aware of the act itself and are shocked to later discover their wounds."[9] But for a control freak like me, every line I carve into my skin is deliberate, and in the moment of cutting, I revel in the sharp white heat that streaks up my arm and makes my head buzz. The pain itself isn't what I enjoy, it's the clarity that comes with it. I want that sharpness to stay with me, but it always fades away. When it's over, I think, *I should've made it hurt more.*

7.

When sharks fuck, they bleed. At least, the females do. To show their interest, male sharks bite female sharks in various places, and once mating begins, they bite the female's pectoral fins in order to keep her in place. A column on Discovery's online "Shark Feed" says, "It's typically easy to spot the female sharks that have recently mated. They will have noticeable bite marks and raw skin."[10] And just because a female has mated once, it doesn't mean she's off-limits for other males. Multiple paternity has been documented in at least six species of sharks. "Basically, the female doesn't have much say about who she mates with," said Andrew Nosal, lead author at the Scripps Institution of Oceanography's Marine Biology Research Division, on Discovery News: "She can attempt to fight and escape, but may incur greater injury in the process. To minimize the chance of injury, the female may just go along with it, even though there appears to be no biological need to mate with more than one male per reproductive cycle."[11]

"So were you penetrated or was it just touching?" the doctor asked.

"*Just?*" I felt humiliated. "Why do you need to know that?"

He stared at me, then made a note on my chart: *Patient was molested as a child.*

The doctor looked bored—all the staff doctors did, but maybe they were just exhausted. Dark half-moons hung underneath their droopy, tired eyes, and permanent lines creased their foreheads. How many times must they have heard stories like mine? Even so, I hated knowing that every doctor, nurse, and social worker would read my chart and know this one thing about me: *Patient was molested as a child.* I hated that this trauma was at the center of who they saw. I hated feeling as if this trauma was at the center of who I was.

I wanted to get away from the hospital staff's incessant questions, but even if I could, I knew I wouldn't be able to escape my own memories.

"So tell me, were you penetrated or was it just touching?"

8.

Three times a day, I was handed a trayful of food I didn't want to eat. In the ward, food was ritual. Breakfast at 8. Meds at 9. Snack at 10. Lunch at 12. Snack at 2. Dinner at 5. Snack at 8. Meds at 9. Sandwiches at 11. Each tray was loaded with a carton of milk, a plastic cup of juice sealed with tinfoil, a small Styrofoam cup of coffee or tea, a slice of wheat bread sealed in plastic wrap, and a metal container covered with a plastic lid. Inside the container was a scoop of scrambled eggs if it was breakfast and canned vegetables and a lump of coagulated protein covered in sauce if it was dinner. The only item not wrapped in plastic was a piece of whole fruit, an apple or an orange. The smell of eggs in the morning made me want to vomit. The afternoon snack of rice pudding looked like actual vomit.

Tiger sharks, also known as "garbage guts," will eat anything. While their main diet consists of bony fish, shellfish, and sea turtles, they'll take a bite out of anything they can sink their teeth into.

Parts of horses, pigs, crocodile heads, license plates, car tires, nails, oil cans, beer bottles, and even a doll have been found inside their stomachs. But just because a tiger shark can bite and swallow doesn't mean it can digest. Luckily, these sharks have the ability to vomit up their entire stomach, flipping it completely inside out and regurgitating the contents—whatever is left inside. They do this often after a meal of sea turtles. They digest the meat and purge the shells.[12]

At every meal, I would eat only one thing, the piece of fruit. I would peel the orange slowly, trying to keep the skin intact as one piece. I'd pull two sections of orange apart and bite into one slice at a time, not bothering to wipe the juice that dripped down my chin. The apples I'd eat from the top down, stem, seeds, and all. I chewed slowly, methodically. For the next ten minutes, I was all teeth, jaws, and tongue.

I learned quickly whom I could give the rest of my food to. David would always take my coffee and milk. The juice went to Carlos, the bread to Joanie. I'd force myself to take two bites of mush vegetables and one bite of lumpy protein and then I'd give the rest of my plate to Joe, who'd nod and accept it wordlessly. It was easy to give away my snacks. Cereal bars, pudding cups, Oreos, yogurt, potato chips, Dixie cups of fruit juice from 100 percent concentrate, and even the rice pudding.

"Good! You eat a lot!" the nurse said every time she saw my empty tray. "We want to keep you full and sleepy."

I was determined to stay hungry and alert.

9.

My psychiatrist tells me that the spacey, dissociated state I often find myself existing in is due to my inability to connect with my emotions.

"It's okay to be angry," he tells me. "You don't have to feel guilty for having feelings, whatever those feelings may be."

Our conversation is making the room spin. His chair moves further away from me. He gets smaller and smaller and then it's as if we're on opposite sides of a long tunnel. I'm afraid of my emotions. I'm afraid of their power. Sometimes a wave of anger hits me with such force it makes my ears ring. Sometimes loneliness punches me so hard in the chest that I feel the ache for days. If I let myself fully feel all that is roiling inside me, I will explode. So I have learned to keep silent, to simmer.

It's a skill that comes in handy in the ward. Because what I've learned during my time in the hospital is that it is unacceptable to have suicidal thoughts. I've been told I am a danger to myself, a high-risk patient, that I am here for my own good, but how can they expect me to be honest with them when we both know that admitting I am still depressed or that I still want to self-harm will mean a longer stay? I am trapped behind sealed windows and closed blinds, under the constant watch of fluorescent lights that never dim, stuck in the same confined space day in and day out—"This is a therapeutic environment," they tell me. *Yeah, right.* The consequence of admitting you're hurting is being put into deeper isolation. Learn to choke down your emotions, and you'll be allowed back into society.

10.

"Nicole, would you like to read the first part of the handout for us?"

The other patients sitting around the group therapy table flapped their "Skills Manual" worksheet[13] as if they were trying to stoke a campfire. I wanted to crunch mine into a ball and throw it at the therapist's face. *How's that for relationship effectiveness?*

But if I was ever going to get out of there, I knew I needed to pass their test. So I read:

Skills Manual

Guidelines for Relationship Effectiveness:
Keeping Your Respect for Yourself

A way to remember these skills is to remember the word **"FAST"**.

(be) **F**AIR
(no) **A**POLOGIES
STICK TO VALUES
(be) **T**RUTHFUL

"That was excellent," the therapist said. "Thank you. Now I'm going to read the definitions for each word and then I want you guys to write down what that word means for you and how you can implement it into your own lives, okay? We'll share our thoughts at the end."

Joanie nodded. I glared. Celeste drooled.

"Great. Here we go!"

(be)
Fair   Be fair to YOURSELF and to the OTHER person.

~~Being fair means killing myself. It's not just what's best for me but what's best for my family. They've been through enough, and I'm tired, too. I want to end things now, on my own terms.~~
Being fair means treating others the way you want to be treated.

(no)
Apologies   No OVERLY apologetic behavior. No apologies for being alive, for making a request at all. No apologies for having an opinion or disagreeing.

~~I have the right to kill myself. That's a fact. Not an opinion.~~
I will try not to say "sorry" before asking a question. Ex: "~~Sorry,~~ but when ~~the fuck~~ are you going to let me out of here?"

(be)
Truthful   Don't lie, exaggerate, or deceive. Don't make up excuses.

~~I need to end my life. It's the responsible thing to do. I will not let myself be talked out of it during my stay here. I know what feels true. I will not sell out.~~

I know what feels true. I will not sell out.

Stick to   Stick to YOUR OWN values. Don't sell out your values or integrity for
Values   reasons that aren't very important. Be clear on what you believe is the
                  moral or valued way of thinking and acting, and "stick" to your values.

~~I feel much worse since I've been here. My mistake wasn't cutting myself. My mistake was calling that stupid hotline. I wish I'd had the guts to just finish the job while I had the chance. Next time, I will. No excuses.~~

I'm feeling much better since I've been here. I think I just needed a break. Now that I've had some time to think, I realize that I don't want to kill myself. Life is hard sometimes, but it's still worth living. I see that now.

11.

At midnight, the ward was finally quiet. The patients had taken their meds and eaten their 11 p.m. sandwiches. The TV in the main area was turned off and the coloring sheets and crayons were put away. All patients were in their rooms and my roommates were snoring. I couldn't sleep. Even with our bedroom door closed, a streak of harsh yellow light flooded underneath, and the hospital's central heating system kept our room close to eighty-five degrees. I lay there on my bed, sweat soaking through my shirt, hair clinging to my forehead, hating the world.

I hated the therapist who filed away the extra "Skills Manual" worksheets, slung her tote bag over one shoulder, and walked out of the ward without anyone stopping her. I hated the doctors who kept calling me "the client." I hated the nurse who kept taking my blood pressure every few hours. I hated the aide who laughed when she saw me crying and asked, "Did you break up with your boyfriend?" I hated my outpatient psychiatrist who told the hospital he was "concerned about my safety" and confirmed my status as an involuntary patient. I hated the anonymous voice I had confided in and that had betrayed me by sending EMS to my door.

I ran my fingers over the cuts on my arm. They were sticky—blood mixed with Neosporin. Already the cuts looked smaller, not so angry and swollen. I wondered how long before red and purple would blend back to a light tan.

Armando Favazza, considered a pioneer in the field of cultural psychiatry, calls scar tissue "a magical substance." In his 1987 book *Bodies Under Siege,* he writes that scars and the process of physical healing can be thought of as "a physiological and psychological mortar that holds flesh and spirit together when a difficult world threatens to tear both apart."[14]

I didn't know about all that, but what I did know was that seeing the colors on my arm made feel calmer. I pressed my nail into one of the cuts and watched as it started bleeding again. *I am alive.* Here was proof that there was something inside me instead of nothing. I closed my eyes and tried to sleep.

Kill yourself. Kill yourself. Kill yourself. Kill yourself. Don't kill yourself. Kill yourself. Kill yourself. Kill yourself. Kill yourself. Kill yourself. Don't kill yourself. Kill yourself. Kill yourself. Kill yourself. Kill yourself. Don't kill yourself. Kill yourself. Kill yourself. Kill yourself. Kill yourself. Kill yourself. Kill yourself. Kill yourself. Kill yourself. Don't kill yourself. Kill yourself. Kill yourself. Kill yourself. Don't kill yourself. Kill yourself. Kill yourself. Don't kill yourself.

Kill yourself. Don't kill yourself. Kill yourself. Don't kill yourself. Kill yourself. Don't kill yourself. Kill yourself. Don't kill yourself. Kill yourself.

I pressed my hands against my ears. *Stop*, I whispered to myself. *Please stop.* When the noise is coming from inside your head, there is no escape.

Just then, Joanie sat up in bed. She scooted to the edge, planted her feet on the floor, and opened her side of the cabinet. The door creaked. She paused for a moment, then shut it. Another pause, then she opened it again. I stared as she continued opening and shutting the cabinet door. *Creak, click, creak, click, creak, click.* She rocked back and forth with the sound, mumbling to herself, and then started sobbing. I wondered where she was. I wondered what she was trying to escape.

12.

I was released from the psych ward on the morning of the fourth day, hungry and exhausted. I had barely slept the past three nights and the snug-fitting jeans I was wearing when I was first admitted were loose. A social worker handed me my discharge papers, and two nurses returned the rest of my belongings—keys, phone, wallet—in a brown paper bag. Two guards stood on either side of the door to prevent any other patients from leaving with me. I made my way through the labyrinth of hospital hallways and stepped out into the frigid December air. There was snow on the ground. Light glistened on car hoods and street lamps. My breath fogged in front of me. I had survived the nightmare, but I still felt stuck in a bizarre dream. I stood there, stunned by the strangeness of all that had happened, unsure of what to do next. I was free in a world full of sharp things. I was scared. I was exhilarated. I stood there for a moment longer, letting the cold air sting my face.

13.

When I dream about sharks, it's always the great white I see. She begins at a distance, swims calm and steady toward me while I hover, suspended in the stillness of the water. Her silver skin shimmers against an ocean so dark and so blue it's nearly black. The blackness stretches out on all sides of us and to an abyss below. I look up, and I cannot see any light. As she gets closer, I see deep scars across her face. There's a gash above her eye, there are slashes along the top and sides of her head. Her right nostril is torn. Red stains her lower jaw, and her mouth is parted just enough to reveal a million jagged teeth. Her tail moves back and forth propelling her forward. She glides—silently. She is beautiful. I am in awe. She gets closer and begins circling me. I shiver as I meet her gaze. Her eyes are black and cold, and all at once I am faced with the terrifying reality and unreality of this world, of the darkness inside and outside. But somehow, this time, I am not afraid.

Tear me open, I tell her. *I dare you.*

NOTES

1. Jun Hongo, "Great White Shark Dies at Aquarium in Japan," *The Wall Street Journal*, January 8, 2016, https://blogs.wsj.com/japanrealtime/2016/01/08/great-white-shark-dies-at-japan-aquarium/?mod=e2fb.

2. Michael Tye, "Do Sharks Feel Pain?" *Psychology Today*, March 21, 2017, https://www.psychologytoday.com/blog/genuinely-conscious/201703/do-sharks-feel-pain.

3. Sherry Boschert, "Stingray Wounds Excruciatingly Painful, Slow to Heal," *American College of Emergency Physicians News*, November 2007, https://www.acep.org/Clinical—Practice-Management/Stingray-Wounds-Excrutiatingly-Painful,-Slow-to-Heal/.

4. R. Aidan Martin, "Do Sharks Feel Pain?" Biology of Sharks and Rays online course, accessed April 21, 2017, http://elasmo-research.org/education/topics/s_pain.htm.

5. Michelle Wcisel, "How Many Teeth Does a White Shark Have?" *Marine Dynamics Blog*, August 16, 2012, http://www.sharkwatchsa.com/en/blog/category/482/post/1206/white-shark-teeth-how-many/.

6. Mel Whalen, "Self Mutilation," Psyke.org, accessed April 22, 2017, http://www.psyke.org/articles/en/selfmutilation/.

7. Karl Menninger, *Man Against Himself* (New York: Harcourt, Brace, & World, 1938), 271.

8. Menninger, 285.

9. Marilee Strong, *A Bright Red Scream: Self-Mutilation and the Language of Pain* (New York: Penguin Books, 1999), 56–57.

10. Anastacia Darby, "5 Things You Never Wondered About Shark Sex," Discovery, July 08, 2015, http://www.discovery.com/tv-shows/shark-week/shark-feed/5-things-you-never-wondered-about-shark-sex/.

11. Jennifer Viegas, "One Female Shark's Litter May Have Many Dads, Study Finds," NBC News, August 5, 2013, http://www.nbcnews.com/science/one-female-sharks-litter-may-have-many-dads-study-finds-6c10848675.

12. Discovery Channel, *Sharkopedia* (Des Moines, IA: Time Home Entertainment Books, 2013), 120.

13. Adapted from *Skills Training Manual for Borderline Personality Disorder*, Linehan, Marsha M. (New York: The Guilford Press, 1993).

14. Strong, 35.

MARGARET ATWOOD is the author of more than fifty books of fiction, poetry, and critical essays. Her recent novels are *The Heart Goes Last* and the MaddAddam trilogy: *Oryx and Crake* (short-listed for the Giller and Man Booker prizes), *The Year of the Flood*, and *MaddAddam*. Other novels include *The Blind Assassin*, winner of the Man Booker Prize; *Alias Grace*; *The Robber Bride*; *Cat's Eye*; *The Penelopiad*, a retelling of the *Odyssey*; and the modern classic *The Handmaid's Tale*, now a critically acclaimed television series. *Hag-Seed*, a novelistic revisitation of Shakespeare's play *The Tempest*, was published in 2016. Her most recent graphic series is *Angel Catbird*. In 2017, she was awarded the German Peace Prize, the Franz Kafka International Literary Prize, and the PEN Center USA Lifetime Achievement Award.

Update on Werewolves

MARGARET ATWOOD

In the old days, all werewolves were male.
They burst through their bluejean clothing
as well as their own split skins,
exposed themselves in parks,
howled at the moonshine.
Those things frat boys do.

Went too far with the pigtail yanking—
growled down into the pink and wriggling
females, who cried *Wee wee*
wee all the way to the bone.
Heck, it was only flirting,
plus a canid sense of fun:
See Jane run!

But now it's different:
No longer gender specific.
Now it's a global threat.

Long-legged women sprint through ravines
in furry warmups, a pack of kinky
models in sado–French *Vogue* getups
and airbrushed short-term memories,
bent on no-penalties rampage.

Look at their red-rimmed paws!
Look at their gnashing eyeballs!
Look at the backlit gauze
of their full-moon subversive halos!
Hairy all over, this belle dame,
and it's not a sweater.

O freedom, freedom and power!
they sing as they lope over bridges,
bums to the wind, ripping out throats
on footpaths, pissing off brokers.

Tomorrow they'll be back
in their middle-management black
and Jimmy Choos
with hours they can't account for
and first dates' blood on the stairs.
They'll make some calls: *Good-bye.*
It isn't you, it's me. I can't say why.
They'll dream of sprouting tails
at sales meetings,
right in the audiovisuals.
They'll have addictive hangovers
and ruined nails.

Fourteen Aspects of Power

BARRY LOPEZ

I.

Suddenly there is shouting in the wadi, around the bend up ahead. Three Kamba men have reversed direction and are racing toward Kamoya and me. *"Ikuuwa, ikuuwa!"* they shout. There's a dugway in the stream bank to the left up which we all scramble. From the top of it the five of us watch the snake's approach. It moves briskly, a thin stream of gleaming water eight feet long, gliding through brush on the far side of the wadi a foot off the ground. It carries enough neurotoxic and cardiotoxic poisons to kill ten humans. When it disappears downwadi, we reenter the dry streambed and continue our search for fossils emerging from the eroding wall of the cutbank. The mamba seemed to pay us no mind.

II.

My friend Will and I have stepped outside onto a deck three decks above the main deck of the *Hanseatic*. A Beaufort force 11 storm is churning the ocean into a crosswise confusion of forty-foot seas. The winds, fairly steady at over fifty-five knots, rip spume from the ocean's crests and howl through the ship's uppermost deck. The bow of the 350-foot ship buries itself in the wall of a wave and water geysers through the hawseholes, bursting against the windows of the bridge. We shout to hear each other, gripping the handrail next to a companionway in the lee of the ship's superstructure. I can feel the shudder of the vessel's hull in my thighs as the stern lifts, its propellers breaking the surface of the water, and then the prow rises through and over the crest of another wave, exposing the forward section of the keel, and the stern buries itself again in the ship's wake. A flock of black-browed albatrosses off the port side holds a course parallel to ours as the ship careers on. Six or seven of them. We can see their eyes swiveling in their heads as they take the two of us in, maintaining a speed identical to ours. Their four-foot wings micro-adjust to the ferocity of the inconstant wind. There's rarely a wingbeat.

III.

In Kalamazoo, Michigan, two men kill a gas station attendant with a .22-caliber weapon, empty the cash register, and drive off in a 1956 pink-and-white Chrysler sedan. A witness says one of the men looked "Mexican." I'm on US 27, twenty miles south of Lansing, driving a 1956 pink-and-white Chrysler sedan, when I see the first state trooper speeding up to us in the rearview mirror. He pulls alongside and gestures sharply with a rigid index finger for me to pull over. Immediately. I've hardly rolled to a stop before two more cruisers arrive, pinning me in on three sides on the shoulder. My college roommate and I, spread-eagled on the hood, are shouted into silence. They find a .22-caliber rifle in the trunk. We're handcuffed and put in separate cars. The driver of the cruiser I'm in pulls a shotgun out from under the seat before we leave, puts the tip of the barrel in my abdomen, the trigger housing in his lap, and tells me not to move. At the police barracks in Lansing we're fingerprinted and photographed.

They talk to us in separate rooms. They do not believe we're students at Notre Dame. The questioning is aggressive, disorienting. No phone calls allowed. I'm left alone in an empty room with a three-page confession to sign. A ground-floor window without a screen has been left open behind me. After a while a detective enters and explains, like a sympathetic friend, how this will go much better if I just sign the papers. It will get worse if I don't, he says. They've taken my belt, my shoelaces, my pocketknife. The ballistics test on the rifle comes back. It's negative. The Indiana State Police have ransacked our dormitory room at Notre Dame. No evidence found. We're told we can leave. We've been here nine hours. The car seats have been yanked out, the fabric slit open, our luggage opened, the upended contents flung back into the trunk with the bags.

We'd been headed for southern Ontario. We could go back to Notre Dame and try to explain why we were arrested. Instead, we decide to just keep going.

IV.

I'm in the kitchen making a sandwich when I hear the bird's wings flicking at the glass in the mudroom. Frantic. A Pacific wren. I cup her gently against the windowpane with both hands and carry her through the open door by which she entered. She's so still in my palms I have to concentrate to detect the pinprick points of her claws on my skin. Away from the house, so she'll have space enough to maneuver if she chooses to head in that direction, I open my hands. She doesn't move. Nor do I. I blink and she's forty feet away, disappearing into ground cover beneath the soaring trees. Good for her. I close the mudroom door and return to the sandwich. It occurs to me darkly that I might have killed her, out of curiosity, crushed her paper-thin skull with my fingers like a grape.

V.

I reach for the small notebook next to my sleeping bag and try to write down the few scraps of knowledge I possess about these sounds, words other than "howl" and "scream," though I mark them down, too. I write "caterwaul" and "shriek" and "moan" but not "bay." A banshee wind. Its swift jabs against the tent fabric aggravate more than "buffet." The shrillness rises an octave, reaching a pitch like the highest note from an oboe. The suction of it sags the tent, then the tent slowly inflates and the walls pop. The aluminum poles bend and shiver. The whining hunter wants in.

We're 161 miles from the South Pole. Minus seven degrees Fahrenheit outside. Windchill in the minus forties and this is the fourth day of this. We read, make dinner, play pinochle. A flagged rope guides us to the latrine. This katabatic wind is why we anchor the tent so securely, burying its wide skirts in a foot of snow. It's also why we go outside to refuel the stoves. A slight spill of fuel inside might catch fire as I strike a match to light the stove. If the flame jumps to a tent wall with this wind, our only shelter would be gone in seconds. The wind is why our ears ache. It's the only predator on the polar plateau. It goes for days without sleep.

VI.

I'm headed out to my studio to begin the day's work when I see five or six Roosevelt elk in the trees, lined up behind a large cow. Still as posts. I stop to stare. A few more emerge. I count twelve now. The lead cow has fixed her eyes on me. The other eleven—four cows, a few yearlings, three calves—look to her. When she cocks her head farther sideways to appraise me, I can see the bare white of her large left eye. She holds me and takes in the others, standing hesitantly behind her.

I can feel the soft texture of the woodchip path I'm on through the soles of my slippers and see the branch tips of a red cedar limb barely gyrating above her head. Her inquiry, which fills this opening in the forest where we have encountered each other, is very much larger, I think, than, Who are you? It's closer to, What are you planning to do, now that it's come to this? One of the calves turns into her mother's flank as if to begin nursing. The lead cow continues to stand like someone straining to hear a faint sound. And then she moves and the others follow, all drifting like smoke into the trees.

VII.

I step from the taxi in a rainstorm on Central Park South well after midnight and am quickly soaked getting my luggage out of the trunk, a task the cabbie has waved off as a nuisance. I step into the club, my baggage dripping on the marble floor where I pause to get oriented. An attendant at the lobby desk says, "Sir, you are not properly attired to enter the lobby of the Club."

I acknowledge that I am certainly not, but counter that I've dressed for the storm, hoping to make light of the protocol. I have a reservation, I say. While he checks I thumb through my last few hours. The delayed flight, the haphazard piles of late luggage at La Guardia, the surly cab driver.

"You have no reservation, sir. Are you a member?"

I say I am not, that my father is, a life member, and that he has made a reservation for me for two weeks, starting today. He looks in his records.

"Starting tomorrow, sir."

I offer that my father was probably confused about the dates when he made the reservation. I gesture at my soaked clothes, the heavy bags.

"We look forward to seeing you tomorrow evening, sir."

I ask to speak with the manager on duty. I ask the manager for some understanding, given the late hour and the weather. He says I have a reservation starting the next day, not tonight. I decide to play the strongest card I have. I tell him my grandfather, a founding member, once owned the land this club is now sitting on, and that he sold it to the club *for exactly what he originally paid for it.* The manager, with a Bronx accent, says "That don't cut no ice with me."

I step out from under the shelter of the New York Athletic Club's awning with my luggage, having waited twenty minutes for a cab with no luck, and meet the bite and force of the rain. I don't recall ever having heard that line, except from an actor.

VIII.

In the basement of Building Eleven, the guide shows me an enclosure, a kind of concrete closet with a crawl-in entrance hole at floor level that looks like a port for a dog. Six workers, he says, were forced to crawl through this entry at the end of every day, too many for anyone to be able to lie down, too few for them to lean comfortably against each other for the night. Upstairs I see a monochromatic pile of three thousand empty shoes pressing against the glass wall of a display case and, next to it, loose bales of human hair. When my eyes adjust to the dimness of the gas chamber, with the guide urging us to please move right along, not linger, I see the gouges from fingernails in the plaster walls. At the Jewish Museum Berlin I will study sheets of corporate letterhead placed side by side in a viewing case. The sequence depicts the design of a new type of convection furnace, one in which the dead, arranged like vented cordwood, can be employed as fuel to incinerate additional bodies moving through on a steel conveyor belt, a process which, once set in motion, eliminates the need for, and expense of, other, commercial fuels.

IX.

Riding into Seoul in the cockpit of a 747-400, I page through the tissue-thin pages of the co-pilot's Jeppesen manual, reading a long list of warnings about attempting a landing here, so close to the Korean Demilitarized Zone. The warnings are terse, the wording about the inherent dangers is blunt. With the plane docking at its gate in the terminal, a squad of South Korean soldiers, automatic weapons at the ready, feeds toward the plane's vulnerable points—the baggage bays, the passenger egress door, the wheel wells. They challenge an approaching refueling truck and two galley vans.

I remain behind in the cockpit, after the crew and the passengers leave. I'll be traveling on to Taipei with a different crew.

The new co-pilot is the first crewmember aboard. He checks my papers quickly and finds them in order. We've met before on another flight. I accompany him on his walk-around, a pre-flight inspection of the plane's undercarriage—tires, hydraulic brake lines, the alignment of the plane's ailerons with its flaps. I have no official airline employee ID so have made one up. Clipped to my jacket pocket is a clear plastic badge bearing the logo of the Boeing Company. It holds my state driver's license with a laminated photo of me. The co-pilot nods at the ruse, gives me a thumbs-up. While I follow behind him on inspection, a South Korean soldier approaches, giving me the "And you are . . .?" look. He underscores the authority behind his query by resetting his hands on the stock and barrel of his gun. The co-pilot intervenes in the same moment that I gesture toward my badge. The soldier examines it closely, comparing my face with the photo on the driver's license. He's familiar with the Boeing logo. He gives me a thumbs-up.

X.

The Yup'ik people call them *ungai'iguk*, a rogue walrus, almost always a male. A meat eater. He will make eye contact with you and come off the ice floe he's resting on to go straight for your boat. If you do not depart quickly, or are prevented from escaping by the closeness of pack ice, the walrus will rise in the water and hook his tusks over the gunnel. You have to lift the walrus by his tusks and push him off to make a getaway. If you kill him, the sudden dead weight of his body on the gunnel will flip the boat.

We're subsistence hunting in Russian waters, forty miles west-northwest of the village of Gambell, one of two settlements on St. Lawrence Island in the northern Bering Sea. I'm scanning the pack ice for *ungai'iguk*. I've never watched hunters kill an animal this big. I know they must, to keep life in Gambell as they know it going, but the sound of the big .30-06s firing, the creature's death, the massive bleedout, butchering the animal on the ice—I'm never completely at ease with it. This is not my culture.

I'm the guest. I help with the butchering, as they expect.

XI.

I'm boarding a plane for Denver at the municipal airport in Amarillo, following a recent upgrade of Transportation Safety Administration security rules. One of the inspectors questions the bottle of ink.

"It's ink. For a fountain pen," I say. "Less than three ounces."

He knits his brow and waves a colleague over.

His approach is a slow, self-conscious swagger. "Ink," the first man tells him. The second young man appears to feel that his uniform and his bearing radiate authority. The men share a look of amused disbelief. The new fellow, standing a little too close, displays a ballpoint pen for me. He says that, in the future, I should consider traveling with something like this, that a fountain pen is not an appropriate item for air travel.

"Are we all right now, sir?" he says. A taunt.

I don't respond. He says the words again, louder, closer. I can feel his spittle on my cheek. He has me wedged against a steel inspection table.

"Ready to go now, sir? May we offer you any additional help?" These are jeers. He's crowding very close but not actually touching me. I pick up my hand luggage and turn toward him, waiting for him to give way, which he delays in doing. As I walk off he says, "Have a good trip, sir."

XII.

It's long ago in Nelchina Basin, south of the Alaska Range. I'm helping a friend in the Alaska Department of Fish and Game anesthetize wolves and place radio collars on them. A part of me is uncomfortable doing this, but I know that without this data, about their movements and their territorial boundaries, the chance of getting an enforceable legal ruling to relieve hunting pressure on wolves in this state will be almost impossible. The law as it currently stands privileges the hunter.

We dart the wolves with a tranquilizer gun from a helicopter, land, perform a physical exam, and fit each of them with a collar. If we've darted two or three from the same pack, we gather them up where they've gone down, sedated by the drug, and ferry them all to a spot where they'll be examined together. We arrange their lolling heads on spruce boughs to keep their noses out of the snow and face them away from the sun, because the drug we're using dilates their pupils. As if it would make a difference, or as though they could understand, I apologize to them. I explain what we're doing in a few sentences. That morning a wolf not fully sedated had snapped at my friend, opening a gash and producing a hematoma half the size of his right forearm. When I commiserate, he says, "Wouldn't you do the same? If you were him?"

We're ferrying one of the wolves to a rendezvous point where we already have two others from his pack. He's draped unconscious across my thighs. Then he lifts his head. He turns to face me, opens his mouth, the lips drawing back. Without hesitating I fling him sideways out of the helicopter. He falls fifty feet into deep powder snow. My friend convulses with laughter. We swing back, find him, and dart him again with a syringe on the end of a pole, a smaller dose this time. We check to see that there are no obvious injuries. The next day, with a scanner tuned to the frequency of his radio collar, we find him. He's traveling with the other two, bounding away from us through deep powder.

XIII.

I've just dropped my girlfriend off at her apartment on East 77th and turned south onto Park Avenue. I'm driving my father's new Chrysler Imperial. It's after 2 a.m. There's hardly any traffic and I know I can make ten blocks on a green light on Park without really pushing the speed limit. I'm just about to enter the bypass around Grand Central Terminal when I see the red lights flashing behind me and pull over.

The officer asks for my driver's license and registration. I tell him it's my father's car, not mine, but point out that the address on the registration, in my father's name, and the address on my driver's license are the same: 105 East 35th Street. And we have the same last name. He asks me where I've been. He asks me what I've been doing. He asks if I am aware of the speed limit on Park Avenue.

"Twenty-five," I say.

"Right. And you were doing forty."

I make a gesture with my hand, as much as to say, "Well, there we are then."

He walks back to his car with the license and registration. I'm surprised by how casual I am about the infraction. I've never gotten a ticket. As I begin to imagine the ramifications and the consequences

I get out of the car and, keeping my hands clearly visible, approach him and his partner to plead my case. I have a slight limp from a sports injury and am wearing a Notre Dame soccer club letter jacket. He asks about the limp. I explain the injury. He wants to know how the Fighting Irish soccer team is doing this fall. I say we're two-and-three but getting better, and we almost beat St. Louis, the top-rated Billikens. He wants to know if I'm going to the Garden on Sunday to watch the Knicks against the Pistons. I say no, it's Thanksgiving vacation. I have to fly back to school.

"I'm going to let you off with this, but I'm telling you to watch the speeding. Otherwise, next time, a drunk comes out of one of these side streets, it might be way worse than that bum knee. All right?"

I describe the stop the next morning to my father. He shrugs. "An Irish cop," he says.

XIV.

Years after we collared the wolves in Nelchina Basin, I'm with the same friend on the upper Yukon River. It's late spring, just after breakup. Ice floes have gouged and shaved the cutbanks and the flooding river has uprooted large spruce trees. One afternoon we spot a natural break in the riverside forest and decide to paddle ashore and take a walk in the clearing there. We tie the canoe to the root wad of a beached spruce tree and climb the cutbank to the edge of the clearing. It's a clear, sun-beaten day. We can smell the perfumes of wildflowers in the air and hear the bumblebees hovering. After a while we suddenly both feel that we should leave. On the way back to the canoe we come upon a dead caribou bull. A fresh kill. The neck is broken, the inert head twisted backward over the scapulae. The right flank has been torn open and blood glistens there in the sunlight. We do not run but we move quickly now toward the canoe. I soak myself pushing off hard from the shore.

PATRICK HILSMAN is a New York–based journalist and analyst with experience covering the Middle East and North Africa region with a focus on the Syrian conflict, international weapons traffic, and refugee rights. He was one of the only American journalists who visited East Aleppo between the expulsion of ISIS in early 2014 and the fall of the city to regime forces in late 2016. Hilsman has appeared on BBC World and MSNBC, among other media outlets, and has written for a variety of publications including *Middle East Eye*, *VICE*, the *Daily Beast*, the *Seattle Globalist*, and the *Christian Science Monitor*. His reporting on drone proliferation in the Syrian conflict has been cited by experts at the Center for the Study of the Drone at Bard College.

CHRIS RUSSELL is a visual artist whose art and writing have been published in *The Believer*, *Literary Hub*, *Muftah*, *Poetry Ireland Review*, and *Higher Arc*, among other places. He is the associate art editor and a contributing illustrator for *Stonecutter: A Journal of Art and Literature* and is currently working on a graphic translation of Witold Gombrowicz's *Cosmos*, forthcoming from Siglio Press. He lives in Queens, New York, and works in the field of deaf-blindness and special education.

Glass Cannon
A Graphic Essay

PATRICK HILSMAN AND CHRIS RUSSELL

Z was a child when the war started. By the time he was a teenager, he and his family were forced to flee their home in Aleppo for a new life in Turkey. During long days indoors, Z became an internationally top-ranked Internet gamer. After his family suffered a tragedy, they decided it would be best for Z to join an older brother in Germany, which meant making the perilous sea journey to Greece on his own. He traveled through refugee camps across Europe, dreaming of a faster Internet connection and hoping to make it safely to a new life in Germany.

"Glass Cannon" tells this story and is part of a larger graphic project called *Farewell, Homeland*, which presents an account of the Syrian uprising and refugee crisis based on interviews collected over the course of five years. Taken together, the vivid personal stories told in the interviews constitute a multifaceted narrative of the war in Syria. The finished collection of graphic essays will feature between twelve and fifteen stories of Syrians from diverse backgrounds, all of whom were ultimately forced, as Z was, to flee the country.

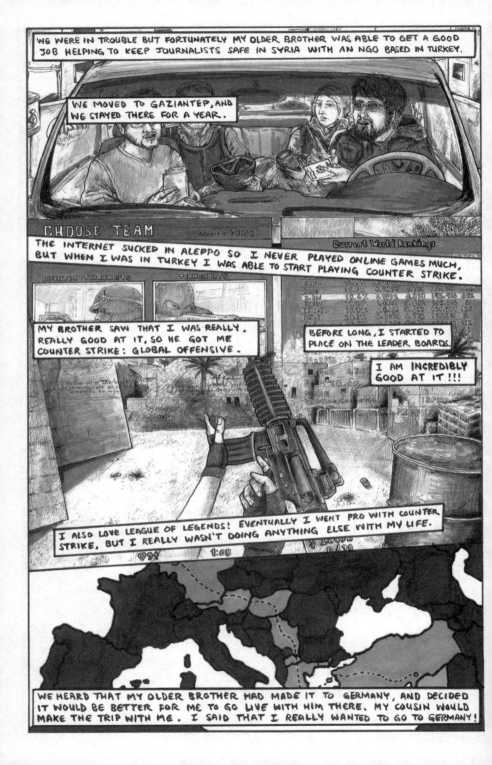

THE BOAT WE CROSSED TO GREECE WASN'T EVEN A BOAT — IT WAS INFLATABLE RUBBER — BUT REALLY I WASN'T SCARED AT ALL...

A LOT OF SYRIANS DON'T KNOW HOW TO SWIM, BUT I DO, I'M A GOOD SWIMMER, AND I FELT LIKE I COULD LITERALLY SWIM THE TEN KILOMETERS TO GREECE.

THERE WERE A LOT OF PEOPLE, CHILDREN AS YOUNG AS FIVE, AND THERE WAS A LOT OF SCREAMING. THERE WERE KURDISH, ARAB, IRAQIS, ALL OF US ON THE SAME BOAT. IT WAS A REFUGEE WHO WAS TRAINED BY THE TURKS WHO WAS DRIVING THE BOAT.

WHEN WE LANDED IN GREECE WE SAW A GUY DRIVING BY AND WE ASKED HIM IF HE COULD CALL THE POLICE OR GET US SOME HELP.

HE LAUGHED AT US, AND STOLE THE BOAT'S MOTOR RIGHT AWAY!

WE DIDN'T CARE BECAUSE WE WEREN'T GOING BACK.

HE DIDN'T SAY A SINGLE WORD.

WE WERE ON LESVOS, AN ISLAND IN THE MIDDLE OF NOWHERE. THERE WERE TWO OPTIONS OF CAMPS WE COULD GO TO —

MY BROTHER HAD SAID TO GO TO THE ONE IN THE CAPITAL, MYTILENE.

WHEN WE GOT THERE, WE FOUND THERE WERE ALREADY ABOUT 5,000 PEOPLE IN THE CAMP. I WAS LIKE, WHAT THE HELL IS HAPPENING.

THEY SAID THEY WOULDN'T GIVE US PAPERS TO LEAVE THE ISLAND...

THE REFUGEES GOT PISSED AND SOME AFGHANI PEOPLE SET FIRE TO THE CAMP — BUT IT WAS A GOOD THING, BECAUSE WE WERE BEING HELD LIKE ANIMALS THERE. AFTER THE FIRE, THINGS CHANGED VERY QUICKLY.

THEY WANTED TO GET RID OF US SO THE OFFICIALS ISSUED US TRAVEL PAPERS.

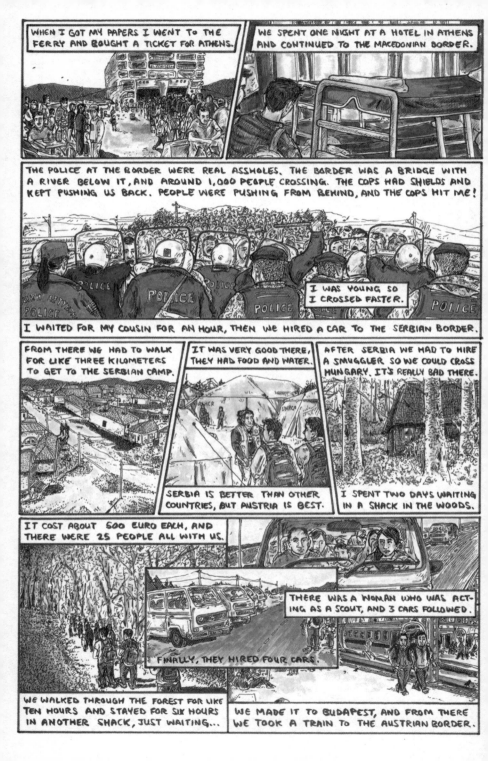

THE TRAIN WAS REALLY SCARY BECAUSE IF I GOT CAUGHT I WOULD HAVE BEEN SENT BACK!

THE TRAIN BEFORE US HAD 100 REFUGEES CAUGHT. WE HAD A FRIEND WHO WAS ON THAT TRAIN—HE WAS SENT BACK TO SERBIA.

I BOUGHT NEW CLOTHES AND WASHED MY HAIR IN BUDAPEST, AND I WALKED ONTO THE TRAIN CONFIDENTLY. NO ONE CHECKED IDS.

HE WENT BACK TO THE SMUGGLER, A GOOD GUY WHO ACTUALLY RETURNED HIS MONEY.

I WAS WORRIED, AND HOPED THAT MY OLDER BROTHER COULD PICK ME UP TO CROSS THE BORDER, BUT IF HE GOT CAUGHT BRINGING US INTO GERMANY BEFORE WE HAD REGISTERED, WE COULD HAVE BEEN ARRESTED AS A SMUGGLER!!!

THE TRIP HAD COST MORE THAN 3,000 EURO BY NOW...

FROM THE TRAIN STATION IN AUSTRIA, WE HIRED A CAR TO TAKE US TO THE GERMAN BORDER. THE DRIVER WAS A COOL TURKISH KURD—HE DIDN'T ASK FOR MUCH MONEY.

ONCE WE MADE IT TO THE BORDER, WE TOOK A TRAIN TO BONN. A RANDOM KURDISH-AUSTRIAN BOUGHT US TICKETS. HE SAID HIS PARENTS WERE REFUGEES.

WHEN I ARRIVED IN BONN I STILL DIDN'T FEEL SAFE, BUT MY BROTHER SAID,

It's ok, you can relax now! You made it here, you're safe!

ONCE I GOT MY PAPERS, I STARTED SCHOOL AGAIN.

I'M EXCITED ABOUT SCHOOL, AND I'M STILL PLAYING COUNTER STRIKE. I WANT TO BE GOLD BY THE END OF THE SEASON IN LEAGUE OF LEGENDS. I WAS ALREADY IN THE TOP 3 RANKS IN THE WORLD IN COUNTER STRIKE. NOW I'M IN THE TOP RANK!

I STILL HAVE A LOT OF FAMILY ALL OVER SYRIA, BUT MY MOTHER AND YOUNGER BROTHER WERE JUST FINALLY REUNITED WITH US HERE.

MY WHOLE TEENAGE LIFE WAS LOST.

I DON'T THINK THAT THE WAR WILL EVER END.

FOR NOW, I'M FOCUSING ON STUDYING GERMAN.

IN THE FUTURE, I WANT TO BE A COMPUTER ARCHITECT, SO I CAN MAKE VIDEO GAMES!

EKA KURNIAWAN was born in Tasikmalaya, Indonesia, in 1975. He studied philosophy at Gadjah Mada University, Yogyakarta, and is the author of novels, short stories, essays, movie scripts, and graphic novels. His novel *Man Tiger* was long-listed for the Man Booker International Prize 2016, and his work has been translated into thirty-four languages. His epic novel of magical realism, *Beauty Is a Wound*, described as a "howling masterpiece" by Chigozie Obioma in the *Millions*, has been widely praised internationally. The *New York Review of Books* considers Kurniawan "a literary child of Günter Grass, Gabriel García Márquez, and Salman Rushdie," and *Le Monde* has suggested that in the future, Nobel jurors may award him the prize "that Indonesia has never received."

ANNIE TUCKER translates Indonesian literature. She was the recipient of a PEN/Heim Translation Fund award for her translation of Eka Kurniawan's *Beauty Is a Wound*, which was a New York Times Notable book of 2015 and won the World Reader's Award in 2016.

O

EKA KURNIAWAN
TRANSLATED FROM THE INDONESIAN BY ANNIE TUCKER

The monkey snarled, baring its canines. The soldier got mad—
cursed the monkey, took out his rifle, and almost blew its head
off—but another soldier quickly calmed him down, saying, It's just
a monkey circus. The two soldiers were the only ones watching the
monkey; the tamer had fallen asleep next to a utility pole, with flies
buzzing around his open mouth, trying to land on one of his teeth.
The monkey kept working, playing all different characters—after
all, two soldiers were still two young men, who perhaps needed
some entertainment before their commander boxed their ears or
the enemy attacked, and who knows, they might kindly throw some
small change into the old sardine can lying on the sidewalk.

O was the only monkey acting in the monkey circus at that intersection. Now she was pretending to be a housewife shopping at the
traditional market. She was wearing a housedress, carrying a basket
in one hand and a parasol in the other, imagining herself walking
along the muddy aisles, getting catcalled by the market toughs, her
butt getting pinched by the coolies, her chest—even though it was
flat—getting felt up by the rice merchant. She often played this role,
as had the monkeys before her, and both soldiers finally chuckled,
wiping the sweat from their brows.

Then O played a soldier. She carried a rifle, walked stiffly—one, two, one, two, left, right, left, right. She held her chin high, imperious. Her fierce eyes stared straight ahead. She stopped in front of the two soldiers and then cocked her rifle, aiming it right at one of their heads.

Bang!

Hungover from his bender the night before, the tamer couldn't keep himself awake. He collapsed near a traffic light in a spot kept cool by the shadow of a concrete overpass. As often happened, he left the monkey to act alone, entertaining the people of Jakarta who passed by.

Even though the tamer had fallen asleep, O tried to carry out her task. If there was a brokenhearted youth contemplating suicide, she would be his personal entertainer, chasing away all his troubles and despair so that he would leave her planning to live for more than a hundred years. If there was a hotheaded young convenience store cashier, furious because a customer had just insulted her, the monkey would be there, like a refreshing wind blowing across the crown of her head, and the girl would leave smiling or even laughing, showing off a row of beautiful teeth. And if there was an old man, chilled to the bone from loneliness and boredom, this monkey would be the blanket to warm him up.

She did whatever she could for the people, even though the sun beat down on her mercilessly. Even though the exhaust smoke from the dilapidated city bus belched in her face. Even though hunger whimpered in her stomach.

A narrow chain encircled her neck. A long rope stretching out from that chain was tied firmly to the tamer's ankle. If she walked too far the rope would stop her, and she would know that she had to move back closer to him.

Just like human beings, of course sometimes she got tired. Seeing that her tamer was asleep, she climbed onto their wagon, trying to get into a comfortable position. She could barely keep her eyes open. The wind blowing through the side streets gently rocked her. Her eyelids began to droop. She felt the world slipping away. She was almost asleep when the tamer's bellow startled her.

"Get up, dummy!" He brandished his whip. "Who said you could take a nap?"

And the whip struck the monkey's back.

A little dog was watching them. People called him Pup, which of course is what most puppies are called. He watched the tamer once again lie facedown next to the traffic light, and soon after that fall asleep with his mouth wide open. His threadbare shirt was left hanging open too—but that was just because he had lost a few of the buttons—displaying his emaciated chest. When he approached, the puppy could smell the man's rank sweat.

He waited a few moments until he was sure the tamer was sound asleep, and then came out of his hiding place in the unkempt bushes by the roadside. He was already an expert at crossing the street safely, going just when the traffic stopped in front of the red light.

"You have to escape from that crazy goon," the puppy said to O, who no longer dared to rest.

One of the puppy's ears was partially torn off, and his body was covered in sores and scars, but despite his appearance he always seemed quite pleased with himself. When explaining why he felt the right to be so conceited, he would say it was because he didn't have anyone controlling him or telling him what to do: he was the master of his own fate. He ate whatever he could find without having to wait for a human hand to satisfy his hunger. He could sleep wherever he wanted, go wherever he wanted, piss wherever he wanted, and bark at whatever he wanted to bark at.

"There's nothing worse than becoming a slave to a human. You have to escape, Monkey."

But, just as she had in all their previous conversations, the monkey simply said, "No."

There was nothing more patient than the sardine can that hung around with the monkey circus. It sat on the sidewalk, waiting for someone to toss some small change into its belly.

Long ago, it had been filled with sardines, preserved and floating in a wallow of tomato sauce. The sardine can had sat in a row with its brothers and sisters on a convenience store rack, shivering a bit from the air-conditioning. They didn't talk to one another and were only occasionally knocked into each other, patiently waiting for someone to fall in love with one of them.

An old woman with a shopping basket carrying a plastic bag full of eggs and a tub of butter had stood before them. Just by looking at her, the sardine can could tell she lived alone. And then, it understood that her husband had died, was nothing but a pile of bones in the dirt, but even so she was still collecting his pension (luckily, he had worked as a city government employee). The woman was going to use some of that pension to take one of the sardine cans home.

When it got to her house and heard the old nag talk, the sardine can also realized that none of her kids could stand to dine with her. She took all the fish out of the can's belly, and they were enough for her breakfast, lunch, and dinner. While she ate, the old woman carped on and on to herself. The leftovers were thrown to the neighbor's cat, who was always waiting faithfully at the window. Even the sardine can, which had extraordinary patience, was overjoyed when she finally tossed it into the trash heap in the corner of the yard and it didn't have to listen to her anymore.

But at least it had filled her stomach, helped her live another day. Now, as it sat by the roadside waiting for coins to be thrown into its belly, plagued by boredom, it often remembered the old woman. Slowly but surely, its own body was growing old too, gnawed at by the weather. Here and there, it was starting to rust. At some point, it would be useless, but before that day came, it simply hoped that whatever was done with it could make other creatures happy.

"Every coin in my belly will help fill your belly, O," it promised the monkey.

The can itself never felt hungry, nor did it ever feel full.

The tamer's name was Betalumur. He looked to be about twenty-seven years old, but maybe in fact he was younger. The hot sun and dust from the street and the smog from the traffic had aged him prematurely—and had also sapped his wits.

He opened his eyes and stretched. A young woman who worked for an insurance company was crossing nearby, and when she saw him stir, she shied away. No woman in her right mind would want to walk near him. Only the flies wanted to hum around his nose, occasionally landing in his hair.

Betalumur glanced over at the sardine can. That was always the first thing he did after waking up underneath the overpass. He crawled towards the can, picked it up it, and peered inside its belly.

"Damn it!" he swore, and dumped the contents of the sardine can onto a torn sheet of newspaper lying flat on the sidewalk. There was only one bill and a few coins, and Betalumur cursed again. He snatched up all the money, crammed it into the pocket of his jeans—moldy because he'd been wearing them for weeks without a wash—and then, still feeling annoyed, he stood up and kicked the sardine can.

The can went flying and groaned softly, but it didn't cry or fight back. There's nothing more patient than a rusty old sardine can belonging to a monkey circus.

O picked up the sardine can and stroked it. The can was her friend. She knew that people threw coins into the can and those coins could help buy her a morsel of food. She kissed the sardine can and comforted it, saying, "Someday, we will be happy. If I achieve my life goal, I promise I will make you happy."

Just the other day she had found the sardine can full of coins and bills. Praise God, she murmured. Betalumur seemed happy and stayed that way throughout the afternoon, into early evening. He went to a small shop and exchanged the money for a few bottles of Bintang beer, coconut oil, lemonade, and some other things that only he knew about. He went back to where they were staying, poured everything out into a bucket, and mixed the concoction with his own bare hands.

Under the pale light of the moon and the never-ending hum of Jakarta, he drank the moonshine by himself, straight from the bucket. He did it while singing sad songs—his favorite was "At the Outskirts of the City" by Tommy J. Pisa—and imagining he had a girlfriend. When he was drunk, he felt he must be the saddest person in the entire city.

He liked drinking moonshine straight from the bucket, letting his nose and cheeks get wet, his tongue flicking all around to lick up the moisture around his mouth. After a few good chugs, he started to get some of the lyrics wrong and stumbled to the bathroom. O just looked on—she never dared approach her tamer when he was drunk. A pungent odor wafted out of the bathroom as Betalumur's piss splashed into the toilet. The tamer came out without flushing and returned to his previous position, burying his head in the bucket once again.

After a few dozen songs and with just a fingerful of his beer mixture left in the bucket, Betalumur began to cry. O was sure her master was desperately sad, and she grew even more reluctant to approach him.

When the alcohol was finished, he licked the inside of the bucket. He stood with the bucket still covering his face, walked back to the bathroom, and urinated again. Betalumur fell asleep in front of the bathroom door, his head buried in the bucket, and he sang another Tommy J. Pisa song in his sleep. This time, the song was so sad that O wept too.

The place where they lived couldn't really be called a place to live. It was actually the ruin of a three-story building that had burned in a huge riot that had swept across Jakarta. Three people had died there. The owner had thought that the fire and the deaths were bad luck, so he was reluctant to rebuild. He tried to sell it off, but nobody wanted to buy it, especially because he didn't want to sell it too cheap. So it was just left abandoned as it was, scorched black all over, walls crumbling pitifully, its yard slowly filling up with weeds. The owner hired a guard to keep watch there, and because the guard was lazy, he figured he could rent out the place to people who wanted it, and they could do his job of watching over it, on top of however much they paid.

At first, a few prostitutes tried their luck there, with a 30 percent commission going to the security guard. They lasted only four days—their only customer was a man with burns all over his body who just wanted them to fan him, moaning that he couldn't stand the heat. After that, a gang of motorbike thieves convinced the guard to let them stash their stolen motorbikes in the garage. Initially, the guard was too scared, but after being offered a 35 percent commission from the sale of every stolen bike, he agreed. That lasted only four months—they ran off after one of the thieves found a faceless woman sleeping next to him, and then another found her riding behind him on his motorbike. They took their bikes with them and the guard ended up without any commission at all.

Finally, a pair of old trash pickers arrived with a cookstove, a pan, a folded-up mattress, a clothesline, and a cartful of garbage. They had just been chased out of their camp on the riverbank by a bulldozer and a flood.

"Let me be perfectly frank with you, this building is haunted," the guard said.

"No problem," the wife said. "People are more terrifying than ghosts."

"I'll take a fifty percent commission on whatever you both can scavenge."

This time the husband spoke: "Half a pack of cigarettes a day, or we'll look elsewhere."

Because ultimately, he needed them to keep an eye on the building and the ghosts that haunted it, the guard was forced to agree.

And that was how the dilapidated building became occupied. Then, a few months after that, a pair of new inhabitants arrived. They weren't afraid of ghosts either, because one was dim-witted and the other couldn't tell the difference between people and ghosts. They were a tamer and his animal, arriving with a monkey circus wagon—one bringing his madness, the other her dreams.

"Don't waste all your money getting drunk," said Ma Kungkung, the scavenger's wife, when she saw Betalumur slurping the last few drops from the bucket. "You should save some of it for your family back in the village."

"I don't have any family back in the village," Betalumur said. He didn't even take his head out of the bucket to reply.

"Well then, at least you could save your money for your future family." This time it was the scavenger who spoke. His name was Mat Angin.

"No woman will have me."

"Of course no woman will ever marry you if you keep living like this! No one is willing to put up with you except a stupid monkey."

Even though Ma Kungkung could come off as a bit harsh, they were a well-meaning couple, but Betalumur was too dumb to understand that they were being kind. It was as if their advice couldn't even worm its way into his earhole. Not only did Betalumur use the money that he got from pedestrians to get drunk and turn into the saddest guy in the entire city, he often forgot to put aside even just a little to buy food for his monkey, despite the fact that she didn't eat very much—two pieces of banana were plenty, with a few boiled peanuts on the side, and sometimes some rice cake or a piece of fried tofu. The couple often reminded him not to starve his monkey, because if the monkey starved to death then so would he. But Betalumur didn't even understand something so obvious.

In any case, one night Betalumur had bought O a banana. He had finished one bucket of moonshine and wasn't too drunk yet when he remembered the banana, took it out of his pocket, and gave it to the monkey. O had just peeled it when Betalumur snatched it back and cut it in half. He gave one half to O, the other half he shoved into his own mouth.

"I don't understand why that monkey doesn't run away," Ma Kungkung said. "She'd get more to eat in hell."

Someday they'll understand, O said to herself. Just like the sardine can, she was trying to forget the difference between hungry and full. She was learning to be patient.

The bucket of beer he had drunk the night before left him quite haggard the whole day. Betalumur fell asleep right after arriving at the arch of the overpass. He woke up for a moment to pee and then collapsed again. He woke once more to whip the monkey, who he thought seemed to be slacking off, but not long after that he was again sprawled out, covered in a blanket of newspapers, snoring loudly.

The afternoon wind was what finally woke him, and he no longer felt like the saddest man in the city. He felt hungry, like he could eat anything. He had already checked to see what the sardine can had in its belly, and hadn't found much small change there, which made

159

him grumpy—so much money is circulating in this city, he thought to himself, but only a tiny bit of it trickles down into this sardine can.

An *ojek* went by, riding his motorbike against traffic looking for a fare, just nodding and giving a wide grin to the policeman who glared in his direction. A city bus passed, filled with soccer fans waving their club's banner, the driver looking sullen because he knew the kids wouldn't pay their fare or even give him gas money. It wasn't an interesting sight. Betalumur had seen this kind of thing so many times before. Boring. But then his eyes fell on a four-legged creature: the puppy.

There had been days where nobody threw anything into the sardine can—not spare change, not cigarettes, not even a prayer. On days like that, even foolish Betalumur knew how to save money. He would go to the food stall that gave him the largest portion of rice, and buy a fried catfish that he would eat little by little so it would last the whole day. Once, he had carefully saved the catfish carcass from the day before, hoping to nibble away at it and suck on its fins for dinner. He had fought his hunger all morning and afternoon, hoping someone would toss him some small change. He hadn't even thought about his monkey—if one of them had to starve to death, he wanted to go second. He would die after eating his monkey's corpse.

After he was sure no one else would pass by—meaning he wasn't going to find any more cash in his sardine can—Betalumur had walked to his wagon, looking for his treasure, the catfish carcass. But how shocked he was when he saw the basket where his fish should have been, lying in the dirt, its lid knocked off. His face had hardened. His jaw had clenched.

He had looked around and seen a puppy chowing down on the fish's head. He had shuddered, and leaped to attack the little dog.

"You shit! You scoundrel!"

Betalumur had tripped and fallen headlong onto the ground, and the puppy had jumped away nimbly, the fish still in his jaws. For a moment they had looked at one another, before the dog walked off, his tail still wagging and the fish head wagging in his mouth. Betalumur had vowed he would kill that dog. "Scoundrel," he had growled again.

"Y ou're dead meat!" Betalumur yelled after he had pounced and managed to catch the little dog. "Satan spawn, whore's child, zombie brains, don't move a muscle!"

Pup fought back, writhing, kicking, trying to scratch, trying to bite, but Betalumur had him in a tight grip.

Betalumur had been sleeping, covered with nothing but a few sheets of old newspaper, when Pup had appeared and started talking to O. They had talked about all sorts of things, and as always, Pup had tried to convince O to run away from her tamer.

"Aren't you lonely?" the little dog asked. "Don't you want to meet another monkey, someone to share your life with?"

O fell silent. She wanted to say something. She had already opened her mouth wide, forming the shape of a big "O"— they say that's how she got her name—but then decided not to say anything, not yet. She just shook her head, and was about to ask in return, Don't you want to meet another dog? when Betalumur had snarled, "Mangy dog!" He always called the puppy a mangy dog, even though his own body was covered in ulcers and scars.

They hadn't realized that Betalumur had only been pretending to sleep. His eyes were closed, but every once in a while he had opened them, just a crack. Betalumur charged, and this time both his hands closed around Pup's neck. The dog gave out a long howl.

"You're dog meat! Tonight I'm going to roast you up and eat my fill of you."

In this city, anyone can eat anything. Plenty of people eat dogs, and maybe some eat bats and lizards, while all poor people can do is pretend to eat the stones that they pretended to boil. The lord of the house devours his servant girl, and in a dark street corner a girl gobbles up her man. Policemen fall upon a sandal thief at the mosque, and a gang of schoolkids dispatches a policeman after paralyzing him with rocks and Molotov cocktails. Flames consume houses and water swallows up the streets while plates gorge on the heads of husbands and broomsticks chew up the backs of wives.

And the streetlights gnaw away at the night, just as factory smoke creates a smog that ingests the day.

As Betalumur was catching that little dog, intending to turn him into his evening meal, some other dog in a muddy east Jakarta ditch didn't have to wait for nightfall to feast on a human corpse. But what does it matter? In this city, all humans and animals and objects and memories and hopes must battle to survive.

All they have to do is eat one another.

Ultimately, Pup escaped the flames of the circus tamer's barbecue grill and the clutches of death—he wasn't fated to meet his end in Betalumur's stomach. He wriggled free, twisting his neck to bite the tamer's hand. Betalumur cried out "Satan!" and "Devil!" and "Go fuck your dead grandmother!" before hurling Pup to the sidewalk. For a moment the dog flailed about, his eyeballs spinning and his snout hanging open, gasping for breath. Betalumur's hand hung limp, blood dripping from the punctured skin.

"Mangy dog!"

Once again he cursed and charged the little pup. He didn't want to have to fight for his dinner. Maybe the creature was diseased, and full of sores, and didn't have much fat on him, but dog meat was still meat, which would warm the evening and soothe his empty stomach, even just roasted with nothing but a sprinkle of salt. He could eat it with his rice for three whole nights, or just two if he let himself indulge, and he wouldn't have to spend any of the money in the sardine can. He thought the dog was already dying, and that afternoon he was a lucky guy. But he was wrong.

Pup came to his senses just in time, and like a sudden cyclone, he jumped up, spun around, and started off running, crashing into the sardine can before Betalumur could touch him. He was surely still seeing stars from the blow to the pavement, because then he collided with the wagon filled with all the monkey circus costumes and props that Betalumur liked to sleep on top of. Worried he would be caught again, Pup once again started to run, crashing into O's wooden motorbike, almost falling into the ditch, rolling under a moving taxi, and narrowly avoided getting hit by a city bus before disappearing behind some bushes growing on an empty lot, where a sign read, "This Land Is Not for Sale, It Belongs to the Indonesian National Armed Forces."

"Damn!"

All that was left were the tamer's curses—because curses are the best balm for an angry soul. Betalumur tugged at his hair, which hadn't been washed in weeks. The passing pedestrians laughed at him. He wanted to stuff those grinning mouths full of trash and plastic bags, but there were too many of them, and what if their owners decided to fight back? He wanted to overturn the passing cars, he wanted to knock the overpass down, he wanted to smash the policeman's head into a bus shelter wall.

Betalumur turned around and looked at O. She tried to back away but could go only a few steps, because of the rope and chain holding her in place. The monkey knew that now the tamer's rage would fall upon her.

Three half-dried coconut frond spines, the tips fastened together with a rubber band. Those were enough to subdue the monkey, to give her hell, to let her know who was the master and who was the slave, to make her tremble, to make her do whatever was asked and not do whatever wasn't. When they were in use, the frond spines would slice through the air, whizzing, singing their savage song. Even the wind trembled to hear it, and the world froze all around her.

They would leave marks crisscrossed all over O's back. At first these would look like overlapping straight lines, then the lines would become cracks, then little trenches, and splotches of blood would seep out, filling them. Those trenches would take half a day to dry, leaving a network of wrinkled scars before the fur on O's back would grow over them—covering them up, but not completely.

O remembered what it felt like when the frond spines struck her—they were only half-dried because that way they would still be both strong and supple—and the memory was what made her back away when she saw Betalumur reaching for them.

"You upstart, O, how many times have I told you not to make friends with that mangy dog?"

The monkey wanted to defend herself—she wasn't friends with the dog, you couldn't really call a couple of animals who saw each other only once in a while friends. The dog would just show up and talk to her, it was nothing more than that. But Betalumur would never listen to anything she said. His head was thicker than a block of wood, plus he remained convinced that the little dog was his enemy who had to be finished, just because one time Pup had stolen the leftover carcass from a fried catfish right out of his lunch basket.

"I'm warning you, O, you better not let that mangy dog approach you again."

Three frond spines left new marks on O's back. Six straight lines, dark red. O felt herself hurled into the air, and she saw the people, the traffic, the street, the buildings, turn upside down. Then everything went silent, seeming to drain away, down to nothing.

"I already told you, that bastard is evil and crazy," Pup said. He hadn't surrendered, and in fact he was still just as full of himself as always. He kept showing up, and once he saw that Betalumur had fallen asleep, he would approach. Pup reminded O of what the tamer had done to her, of the lashes on her back. "And that asshole doesn't just torture you with a whip, he also starves you half to death. You've got to run away from him. If it ever so happens that chain is taken off your neck, run and never come back."

The monkey was lying facedown on a big rock. Her back was still stinging. But, just as she had done in the days before, she shook her head at the little dog. "No. I'm not going to leave him."

Even though the chain always stayed around her neck and she didn't know how to unlock it, at night Betalumur would take the rope off because he was too tired or too drunk to have to bother with it. Under the overpass Betalumur tied O to his ankle or the costume trunk because he was worried that someone might steal her during his afternoon nap. But in the burned-out building, he didn't have to worry about that.

The guard had given one lamp to the husband and wife on the first floor, and another to Betalumur and his monkey on the second floor. From a distance, the golden, glowing five-watt orbs looked more like fireflies. O didn't care; she liked the dim building with its dark hallways and rooms that occasionally had some pieces of furniture left in them, even though most of it was moldy and charred.

"She should run away while he's passed out," Ma Kungkung said to her husband again. "Thickheaded monkey. Maybe, out on the streets, she could meet some kind person who would feed her and take care of her instead of whipping her."

"Maybe she's considering it."

Of course O was considering it. In the early morning when she awoke, she would sit on the edge of the second floor where an entire wall had crumbled away, looking at the city stretched out before her, dark but glimmering with pale flecks of light. She knew she could go down and push through the bushes growing in front of the building, run along the highway, and she would come to a small forest just outside the city. She had seen it once, during a trip with Betalumur. She didn't know what she would find there but she was fairly certain she could survive. Or maybe she could follow in Pup's footsteps, living in empty, neglected plots of land planted only with signs that read, "This Land Belongs to the Indonesian National Army" or "Government Land, Entry Forbidden to Unauthorized Persons." Like Pup, she could live off whatever human beings threw away, or if she had to, she could steal whatever they had. She had the right to do whatever she needed to survive—that was what Pup had said once and O thought it was a good principle.

She kept gazing out at the cityscape before her, wondering what her future might hold if she ever had to flee.

Then the first light appeared in the east and the city began to hum. The dew began to drip and the main streets began to pulse. O was still in her spot, thinking about her future and, occasionally, her past. When midday came, Betalumur woke, and the first thing he did was grab the monkey, tie her up, and drag her to the wagon. The monkey had to get ready to entertain Jakarta's workers, to make them happier and forget her own desire to be free.

"I already told you, I'm not going to leave him," O said to Pup. No matter how many times the little dog tried to convince her, O still said no. Pup truly didn't understand why O was so stubborn, letting herself be mercilessly tormented. Once he told a story of a slave who was tortured by his master, and because he was so used to being tortured, he thought that torture was the most natural thing in the world. Pup was sure O was in the same situation as the slave. Of course, O denied that. "You'll never understand, little puppy."

"Then explain it to me in simple terms."

At first O didn't reply, just looked at him for a moment as if trying to decide whether a dog could comprehend something that any monkey would immediately understand. She scrutinized his expression, trying to discern any stupidity there. But no, Pup wasn't a stupid dog; he was arrogant, but not stupid. He should be able to understand whatever was said to him.

"I will never leave Betalumur and this monkey circus because I'm learning a lot about people here. And I am certain that this is the only way to achieve my most cherished dream, the most important mission of my life."

"Your dream? What is it you want?"

"I want to become human."

A mask. She hid behind a mask because without one she was just a monkey, nothing more. It was only a human mask that would allow a monkey to be taken for a person. And it was only with the mask that she could forget herself, put her monkeyhood aside, and become a human, recognizable to fellow humans. The mask was the intermediary between monkey and man.

Betalumur had all sorts of masks that represented all different kinds of people, and he kept them crammed in the costume trunk. The trunk had wheels on the bottom and could be pulled like a wagon. Inside hung some other props, among them a little drum and the wooden motorbike, and the whip made from three half-dried coconut frond spines. But out of everything in that box, the wooden masks were the most important, because without the masks there would be no monkey show. Without those masks, O was useless.

Without those masks, the workers who passed through the tunnel of the overpass would not recognize themselves in her.

Every time a mask was placed over O's face, she felt something change inside. She could become a housewife who had to shop for louse-infested rice from the General Bureau of Logistics building. She could embody a soldier—maybe a Free Papua guerrilla or a jihadi dreaming of a sharia state—who would shoot at will. She became a songstress who hummed heart songs from door to door. She became a witch doctor who could foresee good fates and bad. She became a queen who led a country without caring for its people.

"These masks, little Pup, are going to make me human."

To be human, you have to walk like humans. To be human, you have to sit like humans. Laugh like them, cry like them, suffer like them, be happy like them. O believed that she would never change into a human being without first understanding these basic things—without knowing how their eyes shone when they were falling in love, how their hands trembled when they were holding back rage, how their cheeks flushed when they were trying to hide their shame.

She jumped off the charred wooden cupboard that had been left behind by whoever owned the building where they lived. It was still night, but the monkey was accustomed to waking before dawn. At times like that, the tamer was still lying on his wooden bench, with a plastic tarp for a blanket and a thin cotton pillow, the snores rising and falling above his mouth. His always left his emaciated chest exposed, unless a cold wind suddenly blew through.

The floor was strewn with food-encrusted plates and cups, fish bones and lumps of rice, upended ashtrays spewing their cigarette butts, and the bucket where Betalumur usually buried his head. O had to be careful not to step on anything or knock anything over, because if she woke the tamer up before he was ready, the morning would end in abuse that would take her more than three days to recover from.

Bathed in the dim light, the monkey tried to stand up straight, and took a few slow steps. She crossed her arms behind her back to prevent them from descending to the ground. Betalumur had taught her that. Before, when she had just started, Betalumur would bind her arms behind her back—that was the only way to get her to walk on two legs with her back straight. If she slouched even a little bit, those three frond spines would whistle towards her.

"A human doesn't stoop like that, Monkey! Stand up straight!"

It was as if Betalumur's shouts were stored right in the hollow of her ear—she could hear them whenever she wanted. Walking upright on two legs wasn't easy. The soles of her feet felt swollen, her knees ached, and her back, especially, hurt all over. If she started to feel that she wanted to let her two hands fall back to the ground, if the natural instinct to crawl on all fours returned, she would call up Betalumur's shouts in her ear, and this would instantly remind her of her desire to walk as humans walked.

"Eighty-three, eighty-four, eighty-five . . ." She counted as she walked upright, across the building's second floor. The night before she had been able to count to one hundred and seventy-two steps before collapsing, unable to get up again for almost a whole hour. This morning she wasn't intending to surpass that number—being able to walk one hundred and fifty steps before every dawn prayer was more than enough for her.

After that, she would climb back onto the cupboard and go back to sleep. She believed that if a monkey were going to turn into a human, it would happen when that monkey was sleeping. And so every morning, O was disappointed to awake and find herself still just the same old ape, with the same long tail and the same monkey face.

"Believe me, you will never be human," Pup said. In truth he didn't want to say it, he didn't want to break the monkey's heart, but he couldn't stop himself from trying to drive that bizarre dream out of her head. "I've never seen a monkey turn into a human and I've never heard about anything like it before either."

"You don't know all the secrets of this world, Little Dog," O said. "There are plenty of things that you haven't seen or heard."

"And how much have *you* seen and heard?"

"I've heard that before we were monkeys, as we are now, we were fish. And when the time is right, we will become human."

Pup imagined furry fish swinging from trees. He didn't laugh, because he didn't want to hurt O's feelings.

"And before fish, maybe we were worms, and before worms, maybe we were areca nut trees."

"You know what I think?" asked Pup. "I think you're being foolish."

At least she knew that there had once been a monkey who was able to turn into a human. She didn't know how many more there were, but even one monkey was enough to convince her that one day she would awake to find that she had become a human, and forgotten all her monkey origins. Because that was the other thing she was sure of: once she had turned into a human being, she would forget that she had ever been a monkey, just as right now she didn't remember having ever been a fish.

So that morning, the morning when she awoke to find herself a human, she would wake up just as any human normally woke up, feeling that she had been a human for years, back to when she was a teenager, a little girl, and a tiny baby born from a woman's womb. If someone—or maybe some creature, like a dog—were to come along and say that the previous day she had been a monkey, then she would certainly wrinkle up her nose and take it for a joke.

170

"Yesterday I was a monkey? Impossible. Humans are humans, and we have been ever since the days of our earliest ancestors. Just the way monkeys are monkeys and dogs are dogs."

But for now she was still a monkey, and she could see the trajectory of her life quite clearly stretched out before her.

"Most monkeys in this world will never become human, because it's not an easy path," the monkey said to the dog. "That's why most monkeys, and dogs like you, disbelieve. But even though the path is difficult, at least one or two monkeys have been able to follow it. Fate and fortitude and honor reveal the telltale difference between monkeys who will fail and monkeys who will succeed."

"And those masks are going to turn you into a human being?"

"Yes," said O. "Just as they did for a monkey I know: Entang Kosasih."

The pair of trash pickers had brought with them a battered television and a banged-up disc player, but at least they still functioned. Betalumur sometimes went to the couple with a Bollywood film, and they would watch and weep together if their favorite character was struck by some terrible tragedy. If the film was really good they would watch it again the next day and cry once more at the misfortunes of their hero.

"Haven't you ever thought of having a sweetheart and getting married?" Mat Angin asked Betalumur, wiping away his tears. "Look at the young man in the film. He was ignorant, poor, with no past and pretty much no future. But his heart was kind, pure, and sincere, and it was because of his good heart that the young man met a pretty rich girl. Sure, at first she was too stuck-up for him, but then she was won over by that sincerity. They fell in love. Their love was pure, and they even got married."

"You're wasting your breath," said Ma Kungkung. "This kid doesn't know what it means to fall in love."

"Well, maybe you should learn from your monkey."

The three looked over at the ape. Many nights now they had seen the monkey passing her time sitting at the crumbling edge of the destroyed building, sometimes with her chin resting on her hand, eyes gazing out into the distance. Daydreaming. Letting the pale moonlight pour over her body, letting the evening wind gently ruffle her fur.

"I'm certain she's in love."

What are you doing now, Entang Kosasih? O knew that Entang Kosasih no longer remembered his past as a monkey. Maybe there were tiny remnants buried somewhere deep inside his body, maybe some small corners of his mind held those memories. But O knew that they were too dim and distant to remind him of the simple truth. What are you doing now, Entang Kosasih? O knew Entang Kosasih was living his life, like any other human being. Breathing, working, and worrying about his impending old age.

O thought about Entang Kosasih all the time—while she was walking down the stairs of the building, while she was going out into the yard that at first had been a parking lot and now was a nest of jinni, while Betalumur whistled and dragged their wagon along. O was always thinking about Entang Kosasih.

The whole journey she would sit atop the wagon, unless it was one of those rare times when Betalumur was feeling kind and let her perch on his shoulder. Her eyes would roam, scrutinizing the people passing by, hoping that one of them would be Entang Kosasih. Every time she thought about the possibility, she became a bit flustered and her heart beat faster.

Before they arrived at their usual intersection, the pair would pass by a sidewalk crowded with a row of carts. All kinds of things were sold there, from kids' clothing and cheap watches to secondhand shoes, prayer books, and perfume to dried roots believed to improve stamina. Out of all the kiosks, O like the pirated disc seller's the best, because it was filled with posters of singers and film stars. Whenever Betalumur stopped there to buy pirated discs, O would go still as a statue, staring at one of the posters.

"There's something strange going on with your monkey," said the disc seller. "She always looks at that picture."

Betalumur glanced over at the poster the seller had pointed out. It was of a *dangdut* singer, sporting bushy sideburns and a frilly white shirt, with the top left unbuttoned, displaying a lush thatch of chest hair, his hands holding a Fender guitar. Then he looked back at O.

"Maybe she's in love with the Dangdut King," Betalumur said, laughing.

"That's silly," said the merchant, but then he started chuckling too. "He's handsome, it's true. He's the luckiest bastard on the face of the earth. Women are crazy about him, so it wouldn't be so far-fetched if monkeys, lizards, and cockroaches fell in love with him too."

While they were talking, O remained transfixed, scrutinizing the picture of the Dangdut King. She didn't need to read what was written there. She knew exactly who it was a picture of. She knew the man who was carrying that guitar—it was Entang Kosasih. Her eyes welling up with tears when Betalumur began to drag her away, O whispered: "One day, I will become a human, and we will meet again. Just as we promised."

Born in the north of France in the 1990s, ÉDOUARD LOUIS has published two novels, *The End of Eddy* and *History of Violence*, both bestsellers translated into more than twenty languages. He is also the editor of a scholarly work on the sociologist Pierre Bourdieu. Compared to Jean Genet's by the *Paris Review*, his books deal with sexuality, violence, and class. He is the coauthor, with the philosopher Geoffroy de Lagasnerie, of "Manifesto for an Intellectual and Political Counteroffensive," published in English by the *Los Angeles Review of Books*.

LINDA COVERDALE has a PhD in French studies and has translated more than eighty books, including works by Marguerite Duras, Jean Echenoz, Emmanuel Carrère, Patrick Chamoiseau, Marie Darrieussecq, and Roland Barthes. A Chevalier de l'Ordre des Arts et des Lettres, she has won the 2004 International Dublin Literary Award, the 2006 Scott Moncrieff Prize, and the French-American Foundation Translation Prize (in 1997 and 2008). She lives in Brooklyn.

Who Killed My Father?

ÉDOUARD LOUIS
TRANSLATED FROM THE FRENCH BY LINDA COVERDALE

When she is asked what the word "racism" means to her, the American intellectual Ruth Gilmore replies that racism is the exposure of certain populations to premature death. This definition also works for homophobia, male domination, transphobia, class discrimination—all the phenomena of social and political oppression. If we consider politics to be the governance of human beings by other human beings, and the existence of individuals within communities that are not of their own choosing, then politics is the distinction between populations where life is supported, promoted, protected—and populations that are exposed to persecution, murder, death.

Last month, I came to see you in the little town up north where you now live. It's a gray, ugly town. The sea is just a few kilometers away but you never go there.

I hadn't seen you for a few months. When you opened the door to me, I didn't recognize you. I looked at you, I was trying to read in your face the years spent away from you. Later, the woman with whom you live told me you could hardly walk anymore. She also told me that you needed an apparatus to breathe at night or your heart would stop; it can no longer beat unaided, without the help of a machine.

After you stood up to go to the bathroom and came back, the ten meters you'd walked left you breathless, you had to sit down to recover. You apologized. You explained to me that you were suffering from a serious form of diabetes, that you could have a heart attack at any time. Telling me all that was exhausting you again: even talking was too great an effort. The previous week, you'd had an operation for what doctors call an eventration—a word I'd never heard before. Your body has become too heavy for itself, your belly is sagging, it sags too much, so much that it's tearing on the inside. You're no longer allowed to drive, you're no longer allowed to drink, you can no longer have a shower without taking tremendous risks. You're barely fifty years old. You belong to that category of human beings for whom politics has reserved a premature death.

Throughout my childhood I longed for your absence. I would return from school toward the end of the afternoon, around five o'clock. As I drew closer to home, I knew that if your car wasn't parked out front, that meant you'd gone to the café or to your brother's place and that you'd be home late, perhaps in the early hours of the night. If I didn't see your car on the sidewalk, that meant we'd be eating without you and I would not see you until the next day. Every time I approached our street, I thought of your car and prayed to myself: make it not be there, make it not be there, make it not be there.

I came to know you only by accident. Or through other people. Not too long ago, I asked my mother how she had met you, and why she'd fallen in love with you. She replied: "The cologne. He wore cologne, and in those days, you know, it wasn't the way it is now, men never wore perfume, that wasn't done. But him, yes. He was different. He smelled so good."

176

2002. That day, my mother had caught me dancing, alone, in my room. Startled, panting, I'd expected to be scolded, but she told me with a smile that it was when I danced that I resembled you the most. "Papa danced?" I asked her. That your body had ever done anything so free, so beautiful, and so incompatible with your obsession with masculinity made me understand that at one time, you had perhaps been a different person. My mother nodded: "Your father was always dancing! When he danced everyone watched him. I was proud he was my man." I had dashed through the house and gone to find you in the courtyard, where you were cutting wood for the winter. I wanted to know if it was true. I repeated to you what she'd just said and you looked down, muttering: "You shouldn't believe all the stupid nonsense your mother says." You were blushing. I knew that you were lying.

One day, in a notebook, I wrote about you: *To tell the story of his life is to write the story of my absence.*

When I think about that today, I have the feeling that your existence has been, in spite of you and, in fact, against you, a *negative existence*. You did *not* have money, you were *not* able to study, you were *not* able to travel, you were *not* able to realize your dreams. Language offers almost nothing except negatives to describe your life.

In his book *Being and Nothingness*, Jean-Paul Sartre considers the relationship between being and action. Are we defined by our acts? Is our being defined by our undertakings? Are women and men what they do, or is there a difference, a gap between the truth of our person and our actions?

Your life proves that we are not what we do, but that on the contrary *we are what we have not done*, because the world, or society, has stymied us. Because what Didier Eribon calls "verdicts" have

177

fallen upon us—gay, trans, female, black, poor—and have placed certain lives, certain experiences, certain dreams, beyond our reach.

2004. In school, I hear for the first time about the Cold War, the division of Germany into two states, the Berlin Wall. The fact that a great city, so close to us, could have been cut in two almost overnight by a wall really hit me like a whirlwind. For the rest of the day I was completely fascinated by this, couldn't hear a thing I was told, was too busy trying to imagine the wall set down in the middle of a road that men and women had been able to cross only the day before without a second thought.

You were already more than twenty years old when the wall was destroyed, so I wildly imagined the questions I was going to ask you: did you know people who had seen the wall, women or men who had touched it, who had taken part in its destruction? Just tell me, what was it, this Europe split in two, this concrete wall between two Europes? The bus bringing me back from school let me off in the village square, but instead of dawdling home as usual and praying that your car would not be on the sidewalk, I ran, faster than anything, my head bursting with questions.

I asked you everything I had prepared, all that had built up in my mind, but you replied vaguely: "Oh yes, that's right, there was a wall, they discussed it on TV." That's all you told me. I kept at it: "But tell me about it, how was it, what did the wall look like, and if someone loved somebody who lived on the other side of the wall, then they could never see each other again, ever?" You had nothing to say. I began to realize that my persistence was hurting you. I was twelve but I was using words you didn't understand. I kept it up a little more anyway and you lost your temper. You shouted. You told me to stop asking you questions, but you weren't angry the usual way, your shouting wasn't like that. You were ashamed because I was confronting you with school learning, the kind you'd never had, the kind that had shut you out, that hadn't wanted you. The history taught in school was not your history. We were learning the history of the world and you were being kept away from the world. Your own history was the village, the factory, the deaths in our family.

999. I was getting ready to celebrate my seventh birthday. You asked me what I wanted for my present, and I said: "*Titanic.*" The VHS version of the film had just come out, the ads ran several times a day on the television, and I don't know what in this film attracted me so much, I couldn't say—Leonardo DiCaprio's dream of becoming someone else, Kate Winslet's beauty, I don't know—but I was already obsessed by this film I had not yet seen and I asked you for it. You replied that it was a movie for girls and that I shouldn't want something like that. Or rather, I'm mistaken, I'm talking too fast, first you begged me to want something else: "Wouldn't you rather have a remote-controlled car, or a superhero costume, think it over . . ." Me, though, I told you: "No, no, it's *Titanic* I want," and it was after my insistence, after your failure, that you changed your tone. You said that since that's how it was, I'd get nothing, no present at all. I don't remember if I cried. Days passed. The morning of my birthday, I found at the foot of my bed a big white gift box, and written on it in letters of gold was *Titanic*. Inside was the cassette, but also a photo album about the film plus a model of the ocean liner. It was a boxed set, surely too expensive for you, and therefore for us, but you had bought it and placed it by my bed, wrapped in a sheet of paper. I kissed you on the cheek, and you said nothing; you let me watch that film a dozen times a week for over a year.

004, or maybe 2005. I was twelve, or thirteen, walking through the village with my best friend Amélie when we found a cell phone lying in the street. We picked it up and decided to keep it.

179

Within two days the police called to inform you that I'd stolen a cell phone. I thought the accusation was pushing it: we hadn't stolen it, it was lying in the street, by the curb, but you seemed to believe what the police said more than you did my version. You came to get me in my room, you slapped me, and you took me off to the police station.

You said nothing in the car but when we sat down in front of the police, right away you began to defend me, with an intensity I'd never either seen in your eyes or heard in your voice. You were telling them that I would never have stolen a phone, that I had found it, that's all. You were saying that I was going to be a teacher, an important doctor, a minister, you didn't know what yet, but that in any case I was going to pursue academic studies and that I had nothing to do with "delinquents." You said that you were proud of me. I didn't know that you thought all that about me (that you loved me?). Why didn't you ever tell me so?

Several years later, after I ran away from the village and went to live in the city, when I met men in bars in the evening and they asked me how I got along with my family, I always told them that I hated my father. It wasn't true. I knew that I loved you but I felt the need to tell others that I detested you. Why? Is it normal to be ashamed of loving?

When you had drunk too much, you'd lower your eyes, tell me that all the same you loved me, that you didn't understand why the rest of the time you were so violent. You were a victim as much of the violence you dispensed as of the violence you endured.

You cried when the twin towers collapsed.

When I bought candies at the village bakery, you'd take one from the package in a slightly guilty way and say: "Don't tell your mother!" All of a sudden you were the same age as I was.

One day, you gave my favorite plaything, a board game called *Docteur Maboul*, to a neighbor. I used to play it every day, it was my favorite game, and you gave it away, without any reason. I screamed, I pleaded with you. You, you smiled and said: "That's life."

One evening, in the village café, you said in front of everyone that you would have preferred to have a different son. For several weeks I wanted to die.

2000. I remember the year because the decorations for the new millennium were still up at home. The two of us were alone in the kitchen. I said, "Look, Papa—I can imitate an extraterrestrial!" And I made a face at you with my fingers and tongue. I never saw you laugh so much. You couldn't stop laughing, you were running out of air, with tears of joy streaming down your cheeks. I'd stopped making my face but you kept laughing, so hard I finally got worried, afraid of your laughter that went on and on, heading for the end of the world. I asked you why you were laughing so much and you replied, between two whoops: "You're just a helluva kid, I don't know how I managed to make one like you." So then I decided to laugh with you, the two of us convulsed side by side, holding our bellies, for a long, long time.

The problems began in the factory where you worked. I told that story in *The End of Eddy*: one afternoon, we received a call from the factory informing us that something heavy had fallen on you. Your back was smashed, crushed; they told us you wouldn't be able to walk again for several years.

In March of 2006, Jacques Chirac and his minister of health, Xavier Bertrand, announced that the state would no longer cover the cost of dozens of medications, many of which were for digestive disorders. Since you had to lie down all day long and ate lousy food, you suffered constantly from digestive troubles. Buying the medicines to control them became more and more difficult. Jacques Chirac and Xavier Bertrand were giving you diarrhea.

In 2007, the government of Sarkozy and its accomplice, Martin Hirsch, replaced the RMI, a minimum revenue paid by the French state to the unemployed, with the RSA, a reduced welfare benefit. You had been receiving the RMI since becoming unable to work. The switch from the RMI to the RSA was intended "to encourage the return to employment," as the government put it. The truth was that from then on you were pressured by the state to go back to work, in spite of your disastrous health, despite what the factory had done to you. If you did not accept the employment proposed to you, or rather, imposed on you, you would lose your welfare benefits. The only jobs offered to you were exhausting part-time physical labor in the large city forty kilometers away. The gas for daily round-trips would have cost you three hundred euros a month. After a while, however, you were forced to accept a job as a street sweeper in another town for seven hundred euros a month, bending down all day long to pick up other people's garbage, bending over—when your back was a wreck. Nicolas Sarkozy and Martin Hirsch were breaking your back.

You were aware that for you, politics was a question of life or death. One day, in autumn, the back-to-school bonus paid every year to the poorest families, to help them buy supplies, notebooks, school satchels, was increased by one hundred euros. You were wild with joy, shouting in the living room: "We're going to the ocean!"— and off we went, the six of us in a car with room for five people, with me in the trunk like a hostage in a spy film, which was what I preferred. The whole trip was a celebration.

In the ruling classes, I never saw families going to see the ocean to celebrate a political decision, because politics didn't change much for them at all. I realized this when I went far away from you, to live in Paris: the ruling classes may complain about a leftist government, they may complain about a right-wing government, but a government never gives them digestive disorders and a government never breaks their backs. Politics does not change their lives, or does so hardly at all. It's strange: they're the ones who dominate politics when politics has almost no effect on their lives. For those on top, politics is most often an *aesthetic question*: a way of thinking of themselves, a way of seeing the world, of constructing their personalities. For the rest of us, it's living or dying.

In August 2016, during the presidency of François Hollande, the minister of labor, Myriam El Khomri, saw to the passage of the *Loi travail*, labor legislation that facilitates layoffs and allows businesses to add a few hours to their employees' workweek. The company for which you sweep streets can ask you to sweep still more, to bend over still longer every week. The state of your health today, your difficulties in getting around, your breathing troubles, your inability to live without the assistance of a machine stem in large part from a life spent moving like an automaton in a factory, then bending over for eight hours straight every day to sweep streets. François Hollande and Myriam El Khomri have asphyxiated you.

On May 27, 2017, two strikers at a factory heckle Emmanuel Macron. They are angry. Macron answers back, his voice dripping disdain: "You're not going to scare me with your T-shirts. The best way to buy oneself a proper suit is to work." He consigns those without the means to buy themselves a suit to shame, uselessness, laziness. He humiliates those who wear T-shirts. He makes, one more time, a reality of the violent division between those who wear suits and those who wear T-shirts: the rulers and the ruled, those who have everything and those who have nothing. This kind of humiliation from the ruling classes makes you bend even lower.

On June 29, 2017, Emmanuel Macron declares, at the inauguration of a new building that used to be a railway station: "A station is a place where one encounters people who are successful and people who are nothing." When he says "people who are nothing," he's talking about you, about people like you. This kind of humiliation from the ruling classes makes you bend even lower.

In September 2017, Emmanuel Macron chastises the "good-for-nothings" who, according to him, stand in the way of reforms in France. You have always known that this word is reserved for people like you, those who cannot work because they live too far from cities, who cannot find work because they have been sent packing too soon from the educational system, who are without diplomas, those who can no longer work because factory life has broken their backs. When I was little, you kept repeating, obsessively, "I am not a good-for-nothing" because you knew that this insult hovered over you like a specter you wanted to exorcise.

There is no pride without shame: you were proud not to be a good-for-nothing because you were ashamed of belonging among those who could be labeled with that word. The word "good-for-nothing" is for you a threat, a humiliation. This kind of humiliation from the ruling classes makes you bend even lower.

In August 2017, Emmanuel Macron takes back five euros a month from the neediest French citizens; he withholds five euros a month from social security. On the same day, he announces a tax cut for the richest people in France. He thinks that the poor are too rich, that the rich are not rich enough. His government says explicitly that five euros, that's nothing. These people are clueless. They make these criminal statements because they are clueless. Emmanuel Macron is taking food out of your mouth.

M acron, El Khomri, Hollande, Hirsch, Sarkozy, Bertrand, Chirac. The history of your suffering comes with names. The history of your life is the history of these people who have lined up to cut you down. The history of your body is the history of these names that have lined up to destroy you. The history of your body *accuses* political history.

L ast month, when I went to see you, before I left you asked me: "Do you still do politics?" (The word "still" referred to my first year in grammar school, when I'd been a member of the Revolutionary Communist League and we had argued because you thought I was going to have trouble with the law for taking part in illegal demonstrations.) I replied: "Yes, more and more, actually." You let three or four seconds go by, looked at me, and finally you whispered: "You're right. You're right: I think we need a good revolution."

BEN OKRI has published many books: ten novels, including *The Famished Road*, which won the Booker Prize in 1991, *The Age of Magic, Dangerous Love, In Arcadia*, and *Astonishing the Gods*; three collections of short stories; three collections of essays; and three volumes of poems, the latest being *Wild*. His work has been translated into twenty-six languages. He has been a Fellow Commoner in Creative Arts at Trinity College, Cambridge, and is a Fellow of the Royal Society of Literature. He was awarded an OBE. His books have won numerous international prizes, including the Commonwealth Writer's Prize for Africa, the *Paris Review*'s Aga Khan Prize for Fiction, the Chianti Ruffino-Antico Fattore International Literary Prize, and the Grinzane Cavour Prize. The recipient of many honorary doctorates, he is a vice president of the English Centre of International PEN and was presented with the Crystal Award by the World Economic Forum for his outstanding contribution to the arts and cross-cultural understanding. He also wrote the script for the film *N: The Madness of Reason*. An honorary fellow of Mansfield College, Oxford, he was born in Nigeria and lives in London. His latest book is *The Magic Lamp: Dreams of Our Age*.

Grenfell Tower, June 2017

BEN OKRI

It was like a burnt matchbox in the sky.
It was black and long and burnt in the sky.
You saw it through the flowering stumps of trees.
You saw it beyond the ochre spire of the church.
You saw it in the tears of those who survived.
You saw it through the rage of those who survived.
You saw it past the posters of those who had burnt to ashes.
You saw it past the posters of those who jumped to their deaths.
You saw it through the TV images of flames through windows
Running up the aluminium cladding.
You saw it in print images of flames bursting out from the roof.
You heard it in the voices loud in the streets.
You heard it in the cries in the air howling for justice.
You heard it in the pubs the streets the basements the digs.
You heard it in the wailing of women and the silent scream
Of orphans wandering the streets.
You saw it in your baby who couldn't sleep at night
Spooked by the ghosts that wander the area still trying
To escape the fires that came at them black and choking.
You saw it in your dreams of the dead asking if living
Had no meaning being poor in a land
Where the poor die in flames without warning.
But when you saw it with your eyes it seemed what the eyes
Saw did not make sense cannot make sense will not make sense.
You saw it there in the sky, tall and black and burnt.
You counted the windows and counted the floors

And saw the sickly yellow of the half-burnt cladding
And what you saw could only be seen in nightmare.
Like a war zone come to the depths of a fashionable borough.
Like a war zone planted here in the city.
To see with the eyes that which one only sees
In nightmares turns the day to night, turns the world upside down.

Those who were living now are dead
Those who were breathing are from the living earth fled.
If you want to see how the poor die, come see Grenfell Tower.
See the tower, and let a world-changing dream flower.

Residents of the area call it the crematorium.
It has revealed the undercurrents of our age.
The poor who thought voting for the rich would save them.
The poor who believed all that the papers said.
The poor who listened with their fears.
The poor who live in their rooms and dream for their kids.
The poor are you and I, you in your garden of flowers,
In your house of books, who gaze from afar
At a destiny that draws near with another name.
Sometimes it takes an image to wake up a nation
From its secret shame. And here it is every name
Of someone burnt to death, on the stairs or in their room,
Who had no idea what they died for, or how they were betrayed.
They did not die when they died; their deaths happened long
Before. Happened in the minds of people who never saw
Them. Happened in the profit margins. Happened
In the laws. They died because money could be saved and made.

Those who are living now are dead
Those who were breathing are from the living earth fled.
If you want to see how the poor die, come see Grenfell Tower
See the tower, and let a world-changing dream flower.

They called the tower ugly; they named it an eyesore.
All around the beautiful people in their beautiful houses
Didn't want the ugly tower to ruin their house prices.

Ten million was spent to encase the tower in cladding.
Had it ever been tested before except on this eyesore,
Had it ever been tested for fire, been tried in a blaze?
But it made the tower look pretty, yes it made the tower look pretty.
But in twenty-four storeys, not a single sprinkler.
In twenty-four storeys not a single alarm that worked.
In twenty-four storeys not a single fire escape,
Only a single stairwell designed in hell, waiting
For an inferno. That's the story of our times.
Make it pretty on the outside, but a death trap
On the inside. Make the hollow sound nice, make
The empty look nice. That's all they will see,
How it looks, how it sounds, not how it really is, unseen.
But if you really look you can see it, if you really listen
You can hear it. You've got to look beneath the cladding.
There's cladding everywhere. Political cladding,
Economic cladding, intellectual cladding—things that look good
But have no centre, have no heart, only moral padding.
They say the words but the words are hollow.
They make the gestures and the gestures are shallow.
Their bodies come to the burnt tower but their souls don't follow.

Those who were living are now dead
Those who were breathing are from the living earth fled.
If you want to see how the poor die, come see Grenfell Tower.
See the tower, and let a world-changing deed flower.

The voices here must speak for the dead.
Speak for the dead. Speak for the dead.
See their pictures line the walls. Poverty is its own
Colour, its own race. They were Muslim and Christian,
Black and white and colours in between. They were young
And old and beautiful and middle-aged. There were girls
In their best dresses with hearts open to the future.
There was an old man with his grandchildren;
There was Amaya Tuccu-Ahmedin, three years old,
Burnt to ashes before she could see the lies of the world.
There are names who were living beings who dreamt

Of fame or contentment or education or love
Who are now ashes in a burnt-out shell of cynicism.
There were two Italians, lovely and young,
Who in the inferno were on their mobile phone to friends
While the smoke of profits suffocated their voices.
There was the baby thrown from many storeys high
By a mother who knew otherwise he would die.
There were those who jumped from their windows
And those who died because they were told to stay
In their burning rooms. There was the little girl on fire
Seen diving out from the twentieth floor. Need I say more.

Those who are living are now dead
Those who were breathing are from the living earth fled.
If you want to see how the poor die, come see Grenfell Tower.
See the tower, and let a world-changing deed flower.

Always there's that discrepancy
Between what happens and what we are told.
The official figures were stuck at thirty.
Truth in the world is rarer than gold.
Bodies brought out in the dark
Bodies still in the dark.
Dark the smoke and dark the head.
Those who were living are now dead.

And while the tower flamed they were tripping
Over bodies at the stairs
Because it was pitch-black.
And those that survived
Sleep like refugees on the floor
Of a sports centre.
And like a creature scared of the dark,
A figure from on high flits by,
Speaking to the police and brave firefighters,
But avoiding the victims,
Whose hearts must be brimming with dread.
Those who were breathing are from the living earth fled.

But if you go to Grenfell Tower, if you can pull
Yourselves from your tennis games and your perfect dinners
If you go there while the black skeleton of that living tower
Still stands unreal in the air, a warning for similar towers to fear,
You will breathe the air thick with grief
With women spontaneously weeping
And children wandering around stunned
And men secretly wiping a tear from the eye
And people unbelieving staring at this sinister form in the sky.
You will see the trees with their leaves green and clean
And will inhale the incense meant
To cleanse the air of unhappiness
You will see banks of flowers
And white paper walls sobbing with words
And candles burning for the blessing of the dead
You will see the true meaning of community
Food shared and stories told and volunteers everywhere
You will breathe the air of incinerators
Mixed with the essence of flower.
If you want to see how the poor die, come see Grenfell Tower.

Make sense of these figures if you will
For the spirit lives where truth cannot kill.
Ten million spent on the falsely clad
In a fire where hundreds lost all they had.
Five million offered in relief
Ought to make a nation alter its belief.
An image gives life and an image kills.
The heart reveals itself beyond political skills.
In this age of austerity
The poor die for others' prosperity.
Nurseries and libraries fade from the land.
A strange time is shaping on the strand.
A sword of fate hangs over the deafness of power.
See the tower, and let a new world-changing thought flower.

Mother's Milk

TAHMIMA ANAM

The newspaper is my friend. In black and white, it gives me refugees fleeing across the border, their hope-boats overturned, their
children limp in their arms. It gives me floods and hunger, cruelty,
ill fate. It gives me accidents. Sadness upon sadness. I pad out my
own story in this way. It helps. I am sorry to say so, but it helps.

Almost immediately, my husband returned to work. "I can't stay
here with you," he spat. My mother-in-law and the servant girl and
me at home together all day. Breakfast, lunch, and dinner.

We had a stream of visitors. Everyone wanted to look. They talked
in front of me as if I wasn't there. They said I seemed well, considering. They were surprised I hadn't attempted suicide. I asked myself
this question many times. Why was I still alive? Why was I here,
breathing and moving and pissing into the toilet just like before?

After three months, my mother-in-law suggested I leave the
house. She opened my cupboards and fingered my silk saris. Looked
me up and down. My breasts, those bulging, uncaring things, made
dressing difficult. "I can have your blouses altered," she said, knifing
me while pretending to be kind, "while your size is still different."

I told God I wouldn't kill myself, but that I would remain
unhappy forever. God seemed satisfied with this. He doesn't like
it when people take matters into their own hands. I subsist on a

strict regimen of grief. If something unexpectedly makes me laugh, or if my husband comes home in a soft mood and wants to ladle rice onto my plate, I will remember something I read in the newspaper that morning and whatever small joy the moment might hold will disappear. Sometimes it is useful to pretend, for instance when he reaches out for me in the night. Then, because he can't see the expression on my face, I resemble a person who has not sentenced herself to life as a ghost.

Yesterday my husband suggested I visit his office to fill the hours. Maybe his mother has complained about me tearing the newspaper apart with my teeth. Give the girl something to do, she's begged him. The receptionist escorts me to the meeting room. My husband is at the head of a long rectangular table. I pull out a chair on casters and take a seat.

"Problem is, sir," the woman says, "Two-oh-seven's penis is infected."

"Thank you, Miss Beli."

She continues. "We gave Benzathine yesterday and today, but if infection persists, he won't be ejaculating this week."

My husband is a peddler of bull semen. Once, we used to laugh about his new scheme. The cows in our country don't produce much milk, and what they do produce is of a poor quality. I remember when I was a child my aunt—the terrible, skinny one who looked down on us—used to bring fresh milk every day for my cousin to drink, from a cow her mother kept on the other side of town. She had learned to drive (my uncle had taught her) and she would speed down Manik Mia Avenue in her small yellow hatchback with the milk jug hooked onto the window handle. Sometimes I accompanied her on the ride, listening to the metal jug rattle against the car door, and afterwards she would let me taste the milk, pale blue, warm, and nowhere near as sweet as the powdered milk my mother would make up from a tin, squashing the lumps with the back of a spoon.

194

"What about the others?" my husband asks.

"All the others are ready, sir," Beli says.

It is difficult to say whether he loves me. My mother-in-law makes it a point, when she's talking on the phone to one of her sisters, to say how proud she is of her son. "I have raised a decent boy," she will say. "No one would have blamed him if he wanted to marry again, but he said to me, no Ammoojaan, if this is what God has decided to give me I will accept."

When we first married, we were feral creatures. After dinner, we would yawn and complain about the heat, how tired it made us. No sooner was the tea cleared than we would say our good-nights and lock the door. At first I was embarrassed, and refused to keep the lights on, but soon I was the one nudging him under the table, Morse-coding with my feet against his shin. We never discuss it, but we both look back on that time with disgust, each blaming the other, as if our sexual appetites had something to do with what followed.

He won't leave me. The flat is mine, signed over to me by my father before he died. I sold my jewelry and gave him the money for the bulls. The car, the television, the furniture, the saris hanging in the cupboard which my mother-in-law hopes to someday pass on to her daughter: all mine. These are the things that tether us to one another now.

There are two ways to get a bull to ejaculate. There's the fake cow and the fake cow's vagina. The fake cow—a complete replica—is made of rubber and silicone and arrived in a crate from Bulgaria.

As I'm thinking this, my breasts release milk. I put up my hands and feel the warm liquid passing between my fingers.

"Excuse me," Beli says. She gets up, catches my elbow, and packs me into a small toilet next door. Without a word I begin to undress, peeling away the sari, shrugging out of my blouse, removing my bra. Beli plucks the pink toilet roll from on top of the cistern and passes it to me. I do a poor job of patting and dabbing, but by now the milk is flowing and I know that it will be some time before it stops. Beli removes the scarf from around her head and I hold it under myself and wait for my breasts to empty.

"Do you think they miss the real cows?" I ask.

"Probably. But the replicas are very good."

"How do you know? Have you ever seen a cow's vagina?"

"Yes, I have seen many vaginas of many cows."

"What does your mother say?"

"She's philosophical."

The milk stops. Beli folds the top part of my sari in such a way that the wet patches are hidden. Then she wrings her scarf over the sink.

That evening, my mother comes to visit. "My poor child," she says, her eyes shining and narrow. She peers into my face and declares I am better, much better. Isn't she better? She talks about other people, elaborating on their happiness as if it will rub off on me. My brother is making a success of the glass factory; his son, my nephew, has come first in the class three examinations; there are fewer mosquitoes than last winter, isn't it a relief? She suggests a trip, hiring a microbus and driving to that new guesthouse in Sylhet. My mother-in-law serves the samosas in silence.

I can't stop thinking about 207, so the next day I call Beli and ask if she'll take me to Mymensingh where they keep the animals.

The place is neat, more like a hospital than a farm. The bull is black all over except for a patch around his left eye. His fever has worsened overnight and Beli has switched to another antibiotic. I reach my hand through the metal grill and he allows me to touch the porous damp of his nose.

"What if he dies?" I ask.

"We haven't had a single casualty."

"My baby died. I fell asleep and smothered him with my breast."

"I know. I read it in the newspaper."

Beli adjusts the scarf around her head and I wonder whether, after yesterday, the smell of curdled milk lingers in her hair.

In today's newspaper there is a story about a refugee woman whose baby was thrown into a fire.

The world is a terrible place. There is nothing more terrible than what I have done.

After we've had lunch in the canteen Beli takes me on the back of her motorcycle to a neighboring village. She has a customer waiting. I wrap my arms around her waist and we sway down the narrow roads that cut through the fields now yellowing in the dry winter air. There is a woman whose cow, Beli says, is ready for insemination. All the words Beli uses for sex are interesting to me. Like my husband, she refers to the semen as *the product*. "We have had great success with the product in this village," she says. I take a walk around the village while Beli attends to her business. My feet drag on packed earth the color of chocolate. I smell the cooking fires, the grass and wood burning.

Beli is taking her time so I call home to check that nothing bad has happened. Was there a fire in the kitchen? Did someone throw himself from the roof of the building? My mother-in-law answers in the tone she reserves for such calls. No, she assures me, everything is fine.

That night, my husband notes that I have taken an interest in the business. He asks me how Beli is doing. "I'm thinking of promoting her," he says.

He makes love to me. When he dips his head to my nipple, I flinch, catching myself too late; his desire dissipates and he turns away. I fall asleep quickly, too sad to care.

If I could speak to my husband, I would say, This is what happens when you are visited by the dark. You are doing something you consider safe. You are not listening to music or browsing through old photographs. You haven't engaged in risky behavior by daring to read a book. No: you are pressing the buttons on your phone, or you are stirring the milk into your tea, or someone has tapped you on the shoulder, and the sorrows of the whole world, the woman whose baby has died in the flames, the little boy with cigarette burns on his torso, become yours, yet although you see and smell and feel everything, the edge of your own sorrow isn't blunted, not for a small, bare fragment of a moment.

Beli says that 207 is doing a little better and that there is another family in the village she will be visiting. It takes three hours through the traffic to reach Mymensingh, and when I arrive Beli is waiting for me in the courtyard of a small family compound. The household is composed of a farmer, his wife, his mother, her mother, their three children, his brother, and his brother's wife, heavily pregnant, her hand against her back. There are a couple of goats dropping little black pebbles as they saunter around the compound. Beli's voice takes on a commanding tone as she explains to the wife that the cost of the semen—the product—includes regular visits from her, that she will determine the best time for the cow to be impregnated, that they have had great success with their method.

The wife hesitates. Beli explains the procedure again, pushing just enough so that the woman will trust her. "These things are up to God," she says finally, and Beli is ready for this challenge: she has heard it before.

"When the old man rents you his bull for the night, you have to pay whether he mounts your cow or not, is that right?"

"Yes."

"And even if he does, you don't know if she's going to get pregnant. You might have to do it three, four times."

"Yes."

"Do you have this kind of money to spare? Does God want you to go without a meal, without putting rice in front of your children, because the farmer will charge you double?"

She says no and then she nods her head.

Beli leans back, triumphant. My milk flows again, all in a rush, and this time everyone sees, the front of my green kameez soaked through within seconds. The women put their hands over their faces as if they have to stop the milk from going straight into their mouths. The daughter-in-law, the pregnant one, stares and stares.

Beli ignores me while I do what I can to cover myself. At some point, money is exchanged, and our work is done.

When we return to the farm, a young man rushes to the gate to tell us that 207 has died.

The baby was late. At the hospital by the lake, the doctor performed a cesarean, saying nothing to me while he pinned the sheet that blocked me from seeing down there, not even announcing the moment when the baby was pulled out of me, not congratulating me when I heard the cry or even giving me a brief glimpse of the baby as he was swaddled and taken away.

When he was finally returned to me, cleaned and dressed, I had the sensation of meeting a person promised, yet denied to me my whole life. I know now that my welcome was too eager. Tiny limbs crushed under the weight of my grasping, desperate love.

207 was expensive. My husband shows me the numbers on the spreadsheet, the cost to replace the bull. Beli is upset. She has handed in her resignation. "Stupid girl," he says. "It wasn't her fault."

I am surprised by the kindness in his voice. He looks at me as if to say something, but I can't hold his gaze. We turn off the lights and lie there in silence for a long time, measuring out our breaths.

I ask for a lift to the village. The pregnant girl has given birth to a baby boy, dark around the mouth, his fingers like matchsticks. She has no milk, her mother-in-law complains. The Nestlé is expensive. I look down at him, naked except for a cloth diaper fastened with an enormous safety pin. The mother-in-law is looking at me, sizing me up. "It was a love match," she sighs, as if this explains everything. What does she expect, that I will pick up this worm and feed him? I won't. My breasts, thankfully, remain dry. I lean down and smell the poor on the baby, wanting at once to steal him from this room, shelter him from the rustle of rats under the bed, and also to turn him on his side so that I don't have to see his little chest rising and falling, so regular, so cruel.

Afterwards on the way home, my body is aching all over, and soft, empty sounds come out of my mouth. I turn to the newspaper and nothing too terrible has happened. Today, the death of my child is the worst thought I will have.

The next day I take a rickshaw down a narrow alley in Gulistan and find a shabby apartment building at the end of the road. Beli hangs against the doorframe of the room she shares with her mother. There is a window at the back, its light obscured by layers of washing. Beli's mother stares out from a pallet pushed up against the wall, her legs covered with a blanket.

I start to tell Beli she must return to work.

"You can't blame yourself," I say.

"207 was my favorite."

"No, he wasn't. You said 203, the one with the white legs, was your favorite."

"You're right. It was just a stupid bull."

"Dozens more like it."

"One bull is like another bull."

She picks up, from a corner of the room, a jackfruit.

"Tell me what happened," she says.

She passes it to me, and I hold it awkwardly. The stem has been removed, and its shape, like a giant pear, is small at the top and swells as it lengthens.

"Hold on," she says. Taking the jackfruit back, she pulls the blanket from her mother's legs and carefully swaddles the fruit, leaving the upper half exposed.

She sits beside her mother. "Show us," she says.

I cradle the jackfruit in my arms. I sway, singing the song that had come to my lips after we brought the baby home. I set the jackfruit onto the pallet and unbutton my blouse. I lie down and turn to face the jackfruit, wrapping my arms around it and pressing it to my breast. I close my eyes and pretend to sleep. I squeeze the jackfruit until it disappears beneath me. The spikes graze and pinch me. I roll onto it, feeling it pierce my skin in several places.

"Like this," I say. "This is how it happened. I was only asleep for a minute, but when I opened my eyes, he was blue."

I open my eyes. Beli rubs her face with the back of her hand. Her mother shuffles on the bed, struggles to her side, and props herself up.

"I own the sadness of the whole world," I say.

"You do not," her mother replies. "You only own what's yours."

I pound my fists against the jackfruit. I feel it break. Later, my fingers will stick together from the sap and I will smell like sweet garbage.

Beli and I make arrangements for 207. First, we watch the autopsy: a knife is run along the meridian of his vast black belly; his enormous organs are taken out, examined, and weighed. He is hastily stitched back together. Then he is pulled onto a cart and tossed into a hole we've had dug on the outer edges of the facility. Everyone comes: the vet, the boy who cleans out the bulls' enclosure, even the cook at the canteen. No one knows what to do—there are no prayers for a bull—so we stand around and stare at 207 while some of the men begin to shovel dirt.

"We never gave him a name," I whisper to Beli. "My son. There was a superstition. We had to wait three weeks."

"Was there something you called him?"

"Yes, there was."

I whisper his secret name into the air as the dirt closes around the animal. The wind picks it up and drapes it around us. I see, out of the corner of my eye, my husband approaching, his steps light and careful. "Come closer," I call out. "We are saying good-bye."

JOSEPHINE ROWE is an Australian writer of fiction, poetry, and essays. She is the author of two short-story collections and a novel, *A Loving, Faithful Animal,* published in the United States by Catapult (2017). Rowe holds fellowships from the International Writing Program at the University of Iowa and the Wallace Stegner Program at Stanford University. She currently lives in Tasmania.

Ways of Being Seen

JOSEPHINE ROWE

I've a face that shows everything. Or I imagine as much: island weather, the race of thought like the shadows of clouds over mountainsides, bodies of water. During long poses I tried to keep it blank, serene, quietly sabotaging the lines between *thought* and *expression*. A flicker, a furrow, the faintest trace of a smile would provoke the question: *What are you thinking about?*

What was I thinking about? There are diaries from that time, now buried deep in my sister's barn in rural Victoria. I reworked stories and poems, polished sentences, dreamed towards endings. I replayed arguments, old and recent; interrogated doubts; worried at threads. I wandered between the rooms of lost houses, rattling door handles. I composed shopping lists and letters, funding applications, emails disputing transit fines. I memorised performance pieces. I listened. I gleaned, lifting details from rooms and from overheard conversations, from the faces turned towards me. I stared back, sometimes peripherally, sometimes directly, depending on what angle was expected.

I thought, sometimes, yes, about sex. Though probably no more than I might have if staring out the window of a train or walking through the city, and these thoughts did not once correspond to the person behind the easel. The environment itself was sensual, any way you look at it; sunlight or lamp-heat or cool draughts on bare skin, as distinct as touch. Though in fact any touching was rare, granted by absurdly formal permission—*May I please move your elbow? Do you mind if I tuck back that strand of hair?* Models typically positioned themselves, aligning limbs to chalk or to masking-tape reference points, relocating the knot of wood or chipped cornice or, if lucky, the tree branch outside that had been singled out to anchor a gaze upon. Or else the piece of fruit one was handed and asked—more often than one might hope—to convincingly ponder.

I am not an overly confident person. Not physically. It's all I can do to stand my full height. I have an enduring terror of photos. There are many photographs of me trying to escape the camera, or looking tense and unhappy at having been caught in frame. At twenty-three, when I started life-modelling, I was negotiating the wake of a particularly volatile, destructive relationship. I'd swapped SSRIs for running, taking cue from a Tania Hershman short story. There was a sense of surfacing. The clothes in my wardrobe no longer draped like hastily borrowed things. But I still found it difficult to be with people, to withstand the full focus of anyone's attention, difficult to meet and hold eyes.

Why, then, was life-modelling easy? Because it *was* easy, for the most part. It was easy to walk into a stranger's house or studio, swap my street clothes for a blue satin robe, set a timer, disrobe. Be still.

In fiction, the artist/model relationship is typically depicted as sexual, a trope given firm foothold by Anaïs Nin, and generally sustained in public imagination. The model is the erotic equivalent of Chekhov's Gun. When not overtly eroticised, she (always "she") might be portrayed as diminutive, a little wretched, as in Chekhov's own "Anyuta." Or, in Balzac's "The Unknown Masterpiece," as commodity, property which might, like a horse, be lent or traded or stolen.

The artist is always male, the gaze one-way, the hierarchy clear.

Narrative convention, fiction or otherwise, assigns vulnerability to the only naked person in the room. But it depends very much upon the nature of that room. One feels less naked, or less alone in nakedness, amidst the not-so-ordered chaos of a studio. Being in a space in which the creative self is laid bare in semi-realised works— all at once subject to, subject of, and ultimately complicit in said semi-realised works—amounts to a mutual vulnerability, which just as often levels out to ease. In any case, I was much more comfortable naked in an artist's studio than I ever would be with somebody looking over my shoulder as I write. I can barely suffer a cat.

In *The Woman Upstairs*, novelist Claire Messud depicts the intrinsic intimacy of sharing creative workspace. When narrator Nora agrees to co-leasing a studio with Sirena, a celebrated installation artist:

> . . . she unfolded for me, one early evening when we both stayed late, her blueprint. Like being shown the inside of her head, it made those little currents, those jolts, tickle all down my spine. This was surely an intimacy greater than any nakedness: to see this page spread out upon the worktable, with its erasures and its smudges and, given that it was Sirena's, a coffee ring or two, and all of it overlaid by notes to herself, tiny, tiny insect-writing possible with only the sharpest of pencils and legible only, by anyone other than herself, with a magnifying glass.

In the three years I spent as a model I posed hundreds of times, for hundreds of artists, sometimes the same artist over a number of years, and never experienced nor sensed the fierce sexual charge imagined in books or, for that matter, by those who asked what I did for a living.

But the conceptual intimacies Messud describes, the currents resultant from *being shown the inside of her head*, never quite lost their amplitude.

I'd started modelling on the advice of a friend, another writer. I had a part-time job at a theatre that showed nightly double features, old films, cult classics. Every now and then there was a cheque for a published story or poem, or I'd be invited to give a reading or lecture. I wanted work that might tuck neatly around a writing life I was still figuring the shape of—ideally the kind of work that neither exhausted my brain nor starved it of oxygen. Chris showed me a small portrait an older artist had made of him, etched on gold cigarette-packet paper: a practice that had started as a wartime necessity in Korea, working with materials at hand in one's ration packs, and had carried over into civilian life. A two-way portrait, I thought of it, intrigued.

I've come to understand that there is always something reflective about a portrait. I'm not speaking with regard to style, or favoring particular materials, or an unlikely combination thereof. Something of the artist's own face or physique almost always inflects the work.

"That's the thing about novice writers," a prominent Australian painter once told me, sparring. "It's all *I, I, I*."

"You mean the personal 'I' or the authorial 'I'?" I reminded the painter that his favorite poems began, respectively, *I will arise and go now*, and *I met a traveller from an antique land*.

"So much of it is all of a piece, with younger writers," he pressed on, undeterred. "It's not like that with painters."

It is, though. It's very often there in figurative work—the *I, I, I*. There appeared, again and again in portraits, the superimposition of the artist's brow or mouth or jawline phantoming my own. Some imprint of the face the artist has seen every day of their lives, immutable point of reference for all other faces.

W ork found me swiftly. As an usherette (and prior to that, as a bookseller) I was given to daydreaming, more than once threatened with marching orders for scrawling a poem onto the back of a receipt. But I was a "good" model. Word of mouth led swiftly to five to eight bookings a week that I'd bicycle between through Melbourne's inner bayside suburbs. This "good" baffled at first; just what was I good at? Affecting movement in stillness, apparently. *Did you use to be a dancer, dear?* What if I had been, the bitterness I might feel at this repeated surmising of "use to be"? But I never did dance, am not even flexible. Beauty or at least conventional beauty had nothing to do with it. From this distance I understand it as a convenient amalgam of physical contradictions, of strong and soft, keen and shadow: sharp shoulder blades and clavicles, then topographical swoop of hip. A stature that drew attention in direct opposition to my desire for it.

The twenty-three-year-old body, like the twenty-three-year-old mind, might be dismissed as being barely lived in, unmarred. Mine wasn't.

Modelling, my body and my face became grounds for constant discussion, but in such a practical, matter-of-fact way that it was oddly comforting. I was a collation of shapes, shadows, implied movement.

I was and wasn't me: a composite *me* refracted by the artist's eye and ability and agenda. What did it matter if I was reinterpreted as Girl in a Kimono or Nude Reading or Woman with Fox Tattoo? The times I was shown a finished picture or sculpture and saw myself were very few.

"Empowering," friends said. But I was not looking for empowerment. At least not through this, not directly. And I am distrustful of that word; it takes more than it gives. I was just looking for a way to pay for rent and books and groceries, and the occasional trip to Elsewhere, whilst safeguarding enough time and mental energy to write; writing being the source of actual power. Agency takes many forms, but chief among these is imaginative. The fact that I could earn a living in a manner so unexpectedly symbiotic with writing always seemed a neat trick, a sleight of hand of which I felt a little smug. Standing *contrapposto,* cadging a stance from Circe or Diana as paresthesia needled my outstretched fingers, or my arm fell asleep all the way to the shoulder, I was, interiorly, free to drift where I liked.

Some models appreciate the anonymity of institutional art classes, where the model is referred to as "the model," and eye contact is minimal. But to me such spaces always seemed cold, literally and aesthetically; almost clinical. *Like a patient etherised upon a table*, I thought, more than once, under halogen lights, while high-school boys dropped their conté and floundered in my periphery, too intimidated to step forward and fetch it.

I preferred working within the cluttered studios of individual artists, and with small, familiar groups, often those of older painters, flagged by the phrase "Artists Society." The Brighton Arts Society. The Malvern Artists Society. The Victorian Artists Society, where my paternal grandmother, Betty, had once been a member.

Betty's house, and in particular her painting room, had been one of the few charmed spaces of my childhood. Linseed oil and old wood and turpentine, silver dollar eucalyptus, the pages of old books—these were and remain talismanic scents, all that's needed to call me back into that York Street split-level, within arm's reach of beautiful hardbacks I was encouraged to borrow, the glass jars of brushes, the sketches and photographic studies of Italy and Indonesia, the dried arrangements of native botanicals. My late grandfather's misspelled encouragement—*Paint with Pashion!*—pinned on a notecard to Betty's easel. Sunlight took on a unique quality in that house, especially in the painting studio: somehow more viscous—*honeyed* is the truest word—than ordinary light. This light flowed as in a García-Márquez story, slipped between solid objects, pressed against skin like ministering hands: not merely *safe*, but *better*. It has held things fast, preserved as in amber. That light was of Elsewhere, I determined, had been brought back, accumulated over many years, through a lifetime spent looking, and it inspired the same.

By the time I started modelling, that house had been sold, its light emptied away, and my grandmother had forgotten that she was ever an artist. She was in an advanced state of Alzheimer's disease, and had been in care for several years. During the liminal stages of the disease, when she was still aware to her failing faculties, and the terrifying treacherousness of memory and time, she'd greet everyone with the same familiar warmth. When I visited she'd ask, *What are you looking forward to?* in an effort to determine who I was by what I hoped towards.

But inevitably there came a point when the presence of loved ones—mine included—caused concern rather than comfort, and Betty sat mute and nervous, picking at an unseen thread on her blouse, her gaze fixed inward.

To what did she look? I pictured her studio, the walls hung with ancient, paint-caked palettes bordered by the dried colors for Australian botanicals: cadmium yellow for grevillea, alizarin crimson for Sturt's desert pea, or the ceruleans and siennas of Tuscany. (Somewhere in a dead-letter office, or long ago sold at auction: her painting of Panzano in Chianti, sent by mistake to an uncle's expired address.) I imagined canvases turned to the wall, the easels folded down, the exhausted tubes of paint, innumerable—a life's worth—her brushes left standing in glass jars of grey murk.

But at older Melbourne institutions, artists lit up at her name. Knowing she'd painted and sketched there fuelled the affection I already had for these places—their break times with builders' tea out of chipped mugs, packets of Arnott's Favourites in the cupboard (Monte Carlos and Scotch Fingers long vanished). Even the ever-present dusting of conté and charcoal that blackened the soles of my feet when I forgot slippers. I loved the floorboards, the testimony they held in their annals of spattered paint, decades of scuffs and remnants of tape and glue, lacquered down with a hundred years of polish. If there was an aspect of modelling I was guilty of romanticising, it was this olfactory romance.

Head notes: blue gum, lemon, bergamot, rosin.
Heart notes: instant coffee, cinnamon, linseed oil.
Base notes: woodsmoke, polished jarrah, worn leather, charcoal.

I often spent my longer poses revisiting Betty's York Street house, trailing from room to room where everything was always in place, right down to the paua-shell button, broken in half, on the bathroom windowsill; the near-full pack of ancient, speckled cigarettes tucked into a desk drawer (my grandfather's? his last?); the high, linen-heaped beds that my sister and I would sleep in when we stayed. Beneath these, glass display cases lined with butterflies, beautiful and morbidly alluring, the abandoned hobby of an uncle now living in Ireland. Huge iridescent Australian birdwings and Ulysses swallowtails that I tried to find in living vibrancy at the Melbourne Zoo. Along the hallway, carved Japanese folding screens and chiaroscuro portraits, faces emerging from velvety black as if from dark water. The old hound on his last legs, snoozing ad infinitum on the cool tiles of the laundry. The grandfather clock still by the bureau, still chiming Westminster quarters towards the immense, heavy-framed reproduction of *The Battle of the Amazons*, the bridge in the foreground fantastic with gored bodies and muscular horses, all froth and rolling eye, plunging into the river where thick-armed women wailed and reached, a skyline on fire in the distance.

Though it was long since sold, no doubt renovated beyond the heart's recognition, I counted this house as inheritance—the house, and its light, the promise of the world it contained. Recalling it in vivid detail was a matter of safekeeping.

Sometimes I drifted further out, rudderless, to places I'd not seen or thought about in many years. Over longer, painful poses this mental drift was necessary, a vast interior refuge from physical discomfort.

Nothing is comfortable in the second hour. When working with sculptors, especially, a model returns to the same pose over the course of several days or weeks, holding it for twenty or thirty minutes. A poorly considered pose might not show its teeth until the second or third innings, followed by a dread of being trapped in it for all the hours to come. There are brief intervals to stretch, to coax blood back towards numb hands and feet. But in returning to position, pain courses back with ever-increasing speed. It's all you can do to sink down into some other state, leaving discomfort far up at the surface of your body. Of course such simple, prepositional language is not ideal, but it felt most like sinking, like plunging—also with increasing velocity—into temporal silt. Some inner Mariana Trench where all was kept, fathoms beneath the depth-sounding of daily awareness. Every twenty minutes the timer would wrench me back up, sometimes shockingly, and I would spend the short break re-acclimating to present circumstance, decompressing.

But in realigning my limbs to chalk marks and the directions of artists, whatever it was would be waiting for me, the way you become tangled in the trailing threads of a previous night's dreams simply by placing head against pillow.

As with dreams, I often wasn't ready for who or what might find me inside those prolonged stillnesses. My mother, of course, usually in pre-cancer visage (she would be happy to know), whose face occasionally stared back at me, impassively, from the canvases of strangers.

As paresthesia crept in, I would think also of my maternal grandmother, who died of motor neuron disease the year I was born. (The mother my mother would sometimes cry for, when she herself became terminally ill.) MND is often heralded by a seemingly innocuous incident: a dropped cup, a missed step. How it started for Edith: she fell skipping rope, in the words of my older sisters. Also an artist, Edith had continued painting by mouth for a while, after the disease had taken the use of her hands, until that too became impossible. She died within two years, at fifty-eight.

Studies indicate a genetic link in 5 to 10 percent of cases of MND—around that of breast cancer—with a tendency to skip a generation. As with breast cancer, a test for this faulty gene exists, but I know better than to take it. Imagination already outstrips reason. Sometimes my body auditions a strange twitch or tremor, and there is the apparition of Edith. A flicker visits my left eyelid, hardly visible to others even when I point it out, but from this side it is an unnerving stammer of light and shadow, as if traveling fast along a tree-dappled stretch of road, or standing beside an analogue film projector. Or my mouth refuses to co-operate, mangling the most basic and familiar of phrases, words falling apart like soft biscuits. Or my hands become slow and stupid, and my handwriting deteriorates, the fact of it evident in the comparison of this summer's notebook with last winter's.

Innocuous things. Trivial, temporary gripes. I know. But *she fell skipping rope*. Such familial lore has the powerful undercurrent of prophecy.

But the mercenary stillness of modelling I came to appreciate, and then to depend upon. I saved up my thinking for it. Difficult decisions, stubborn stories, what to make of how X had said Y. What other work allowed for that freedom of thought?

And all the while I was learning a trade, and being taught by one. In Melbourne, then and now, the Life Modelling Society acts somewhere between union and agency. Members are added to a lo-fi quarterly spreadsheet that gives their first name or pseudonym, age, height, phone number, years of experience, and up to seven words to describe their appearance (*long-limbed, lithe, classical features*). Artists and institutions pay a nominal fee to receive this list, in hard copy, generally on colored craft-paper. The list was sent along with a Code of Conduct for artists and models both, outlining minimum rates of pay, fair working conditions, etiquette, and cautioning against unauthorised photography, unwarranted physical contact, or dubious requests.

A dubious request might be erotic poses with the artist's wife (yes, *always* the wife). Or the artist might have been inconsiderate of a model's privacy in changing, or become hostile when refused a physically harmful pose. There were those artists who seemed to fancy themselves modern Schieles, emulation which seemed more sadistic than an artistic imperative.

"You have to suffer for my art," one artist had joked when I mentioned that his studio was ice-cold.

"Not for thirty dollars an hour."

The artists and organizations on the mailing lists were mostly known and trusted. If a model had a discomforting experience, a general notification went out, and the artist in question might be blacklisted:

An individual named [A] has contacted some models stating he is a "naturalist" (refer to email below) and asking whether the model would be okay with him being nude while he draws. Higher modelling rates were offered. While of course it is entirely at your discretion who you accept work from, [we] neverthe-less caution models **against** *accepting this kind of work, as it is highly likely this individual has more in mind than just drawing.*

The lists occasionally wandered beyond known entities. But most of the creeps could be identified and deflected in an initial phone call, the audible difference between typical artistic awkwardness and outright perversion something I figured myself finely tuned to. Anything that arrived by text was better ignored:

I'm sure you're very beautiful but I could make you look hot.
Would be happy to swap prints for time.
Could you first send me pictures of . . .

More often, though, the experience landed somewhere between unremarkable and ameliorating. .

Anne ran a small class out of her Port Melbourne cottage, where open-plan kitchen melded into an art studio. She took great satis-faction in preparing an elaborate meal for everyone to share in the lunch break. There were weeks when I was racing between so many jobs that I practically lived on arrowroot biscuits and weak tea. Never at Anne's, where there were fresh salads, dense breads, sliced pears fanned alongside soft cheeses, bowls of comforting ratatouille or laksa, wine in the evenings. The large windows looked onto a lush herb garden, and over a long pose bands of sun slid across my skin like slow, warm balm, making me sleepy as a cat, and Anne's own cats—Audrey and Claude—would pad in from the rosemary and settle close to me for a share of attention. Sometimes I couldn't believe this was "work."

All of my sessions with Neil began with tea steeping while I changed from street clothes to robe. Each week a different blend would be waiting—smoky and rich, or bright and tart, picked out especially from a fancy shop nearby. Before starting on painting, we'd talk about the intervening week, what we were reading, music and films and exhibitions, his plans for knocking out walls and making an artist-run gallery of the warren-like studios we were in (which he eventually did).

His were amongst the few paintings I recognized myself in. (Whether that had more to do with a growing familiarity with the reportedly elusive planes of my face, or with that of the interior self, it's impossible to say, other than to acknowledge the trajectory existed.)

Life-modelling is, for most, interim work, wolf-from-door work, in that way akin to cab driving (which both of my parents had done, when fit for work). And as in cab driving, this assumed transience lends further to its unintentional intimacies, its accidental revelations: a model may as well be a cab driver for all that she or he is explicitly told, or otherwise overhears, being confused for part of the furniture. Modelling in private houses I felt, at times, like a spy, or a cat burglar. That if these people knew the extent to which I mirrored their gaze, their efforts at depiction, they would never invite me into their homes.

An incomplete list of minor thefts for stories, written and not: certain affirmations scrawled onto bathroom mirrors; windows papered over with decade-old newsprint, sunlight diffused in high-lignan yellow; how she talks to her sister; Torrit grey; ominous collections (bones, dolls, a roadkill fox in a freezer chest); peculiar superstitions;

217

his disdainful (violent) shoeprint over the drawing that didn't work out; a piebald rabbit with a foot fetish; certain labels blaring from medicine cabinet shelves; faith for older women in men's shirts with paint on the sleeves; how he speaks of his children; certain messages on cork boards; a blue Velcro wrist brace; certain views to certain rooftops; a sparrow dropping into its flight like a stone.

In a marble-floored mansion in Kew I sometimes modelled for a pair of stifled but not untalented housewives, whose tea-break conversations did not generally include or acknowledge me. I didn't much mind. Of their faces I remember nothing, but of the house there remains a tactile sense-memory of cool underfoot, wet leaves, the museum-echo of the women's murmured voices. So much space and no studio: I posed in the living area, orienting my stance so as to face an enclosed garden. Glassed-in greenery, white pebbles, a chōzubachi water feature, whose plashing reached in through an open window.

I wrote very well there. Or *composed*, if you like, staring out into that manicured terrarium. (Do they rake their own gravel? I wondered. Isn't that the point?) But mostly I was thinking about birds, about anatomical language around the mechanics of flight. About stillness, non-voluntary, as in the aftermath of disaster. *Did you use to be a dancer?* I was thinking about both grandmothers. Accumulating fragments. After the first session in that house, I went straight to a news agency, bought a cheap exercise book, and began the manuscript that earned my first writing grant.

A nother year of this, of tempering stamina, intense physicality entwined with acute interiority. On a midwinter evening in my second year of modelling, I took a tram to a foundry across the city for a late booking with a well-known sculptor. The previous model had fallen through, an assistant explained on the phone. Three hours' pay for twenty minutes. No, not for the sculptor himself, but a small group of novices. Other particulars were vague.

I was travelling to Berlin at the end of that week, to sleep on a friend's floor in Kreuzberg for a month. I was grateful for the extra cash, but the pay seemed suspiciously high.

No photographs, the assistant assured me.

I arrived near dusk, at what looked like the repurposed set from a Greenaway or Von Trier film. In the foundry's forecourt, a long, elaborately set table encased vitrine-like in a clear plastic marquee. A blur of flowers and lit candles and stemware and white linen, the image warping as the evening breeze rippled the thick transparent walls. Jørgen Leth might have appeared at any moment, tuxedo-clad, nursing a bottle of Chablis and monologuing before an enormous plate of fish. Past the marquee, the roller door to the foundry was pulled up, and beyond this one could hear the roaring of its furnace.

No one came to meet me. I moved towards the sound with a dreamlike trepidation. In a farther corner of the building, a small group stood with faces firelit, the sculptor delivering a furnace-side talk. A few workers demonstrated aspects of the casting process, pouring molten—bronze? likely bronze—into a mould.

An assistant noticed me and broke away to usher me up a metal gantry (here: the absurd thought of spooked horses refusing to climb stairs) to a loft studio set up art-class style with trestle tables and chairs and small blocks of damp clay. They'd be up in just a few minutes, she explained. Did I want anything—Canapés? Champagne? A space to change was apparently an afterthought. Directed to a cavernous unlit storeroom at the far end of the studio, I undressed in the dark amidst giant plaster forms—abandoned works, or those in progress, I could not tell. The floor was blanketed with an inch of clay and plaster dust. I undressed on tiptoe, folding each item of clothing carefully into my bag as soon as I took it off.

Later, from one of the foundry workers, I learned the prerequisite net worth for invitees that night. Heads of successful companies, each having amassed such and such a fortune by age forty. How many zeroes was it? A considerable number of zeroes.

The idea was that the honored (i.e., wealthy) guests and their plus-ones would arrive from touring the foundry for—surprise!—a pre-dinner sculpting lesson, and I would be there—surprise!—like a showgirl sprung from an oversized cake.

I felt a little sick. Sipping mineral water from a champagne flute, I waited, entertaining the urge to bolt. Then it was too late. Voices, and the cautious tread of dress shoes upon the gantry, and by the time they had filed in, one by one, I was standing on a chair, holding a pose I figured as "achievable" while at the same time uncharacteristically defensive: one arm held across my stomach, eyes fixed on the far wall.

The sculptor stood unnervingly close while delivering a rousing little speech, in which he illuminated the struggles inherent in life as an artist but added that throughout this very difficult and often dispiriting etc. etc. journey, one of the saving graces was the opportunity to stare openly at beautiful women. Like Josephine here.

I kept my eyes fixed on the far wall. In this instance, I wished nobody had used my name.

Not that my name did a great deal to humanize me in that space. The (surprised!) guests warily approached their portions of clay. Several of the women appeared oddly scandalized for Patrons of Art, if that's what they were being courted as, and I was peripherally aware of their reproachful looks, somehow worse than leering. Though, of course, there was leering too.

The CEOs and CEO-plus-ones kneaded their lumps of clay into vaguely human forms, most with the performative irreverence of those above not being good at things. An assistant charged with documentation flitted between stations with a digital camera. I broke pose to lean down to remind her to leave me out of frame, then returned to position. High up in the barred room of my head, I was attempting to think myself elsewhere, but was tethered by the usual physiology of anxiety—the fast blood, the nausea, rabbit-kicking heart. I tried to reason myself calm, alternating between reassurance and remonstration. This was not awful. It was merely absurd, and not deserving of panic. I catalogued proper, previously lived awfulness against this comparatively benign twenty minutes. This was not childish helplessness in the face of household violence, police interventions, terminal illness. This was not weeks sealed up in airtight dread. This was not, say, being thrown bodily from an angry boyfriend's porch.

You've had it so much worse: an inelegant, unreliable meter.

But it nearly worked. My pulse slowed a beat. This was only a room full of the wrong sort of people, giving me the wrong sort of look. The wrong kind of objectification—the kind that most people presumed my job consisted of.

Then one of the older men came very close, his face level with my knees, a lingering appraisement that travelled from my toes to my face.

Nice, he concluded.

I held still. He went away. I flicked a glance at the timer. Eight minutes, may as well have been eight years. The assistant flitted past again with her camera and I broke pose, leaning down to tell her I'd have to get down now.

"Oh, but we're only . . . okay." She saw something in my face, and broke off. I pulled my robe on and moved as calmly as I could to the door at the end of the studio, the sculpture morgue now as good as a sanctuary.

The heavy door blocked out light and muffled voices; I exhaled into the darkness, and began dressing very slowly, partly to spare my clothes dust, partly to allow for the studio to empty.

The sculptor opened the door when I had one leg in my jeans. He stood there, backlit, hundred-dollar note in hand.

"I'm getting changed."

"Right. You were great, we'll have you back to do more of this—"

"I am never doing this again."

"Well, not exactly this . . . but—"

"I'm getting changed. Could you please . . ."

"Oh, righto. Well, we'll be in touch."

Finally he closed the door. I waited long enough for my eyes to adjust. In the dim all was pewter and moon colored, a lunar-scape of half-formed ideas, and I was still thrumming with fury, half at myself: for not being a swifter judge of character, for taking the job in the first place. For standing mute and motionless a moment longer than I should have, allowing that reptile to appraise me.

Nice.

I could have garrotted him with the clay cut-off wire.

When I emerged, the studio was empty. Everyone presumably retired to the plastic marquee for dinner, leaving behind a woeful little army of clay humanoid stalagmites. At the foot of the gantry, repelled by the clinking of glassware and laughter, I slipped back towards the back of the workshop, where the foundry workers stood around with beers cracked, lighting smokes beside the cooling furnace.

"You okay?" one of them asked. "That looked . . . a bit rough."

"I could do with one of those."

He offered the packet, a light. "Saw some real masterpieces up there," he added, brows raised.

They found me a chair, offered beer from their ice bucket, a literal place by the literal fire. Most were artists themselves, working partly for access to the foundry and materials. I let my satchel drop onto the shop floor and listened as they lambasted the sculptor (for my sake or theirs—who knew?).

"You know, every time he finishes a sculpture, he has it documented with a naked girl draped across it."

"Like a muscle car calendar."

The anxious charge in my blood gradually died down. I stopped shaking. I regained enough of my voice to laugh with them. But there was only so much satisfaction in having misgivings about the pairing of art and wealth—that the absence of any financial risk tends to stymie something vital in the way of discernment—so violently reinforced.

Riding the tram home that night, all the nourishing aspects of the work were temporarily blotted out: the easy conversations over tea, the companionable weight of sleepy cats, my own gentler reassessment of my body and how it should look, the intoxicating smell of wood under a hundred years of polish and the rooms it led me back through.

After Berlin, I decided as the tram swayed over the river. After Berlin, I would never do this again.

There was a job in the morning, my last before leaving the country, and I wanted to cancel it. But the artist was a soft-spoken man I'd worked with for several months, whose studio was out the back of his family home. He had an old world still-life style, familiar and texturally comforting, somehow representative of the man himself.

I went, under-slept, less talkative than usual. And the quiet hours in his studio dissolved some of the previous night's bitterness.

"There's a little extra," Michael said, when handing me my fee. Almost shyly, he told me this, as though afraid of it being taken the wrong way. "Just, I'd like to shout you a meal in Berlin."

It wasn't a huge amount, not a grand proprietorial gesture. It was the modest kindness of a man who had once been young and broke in Europe, and it restored some of the faith I had for the work.

I went back to modelling after Berlin, and was working with Michael when my father's wife called about my grandmother. Betty had died in the night.

Michael gently put down his brushes and gave me a few minutes alone. I sat on the chaise, robe drawn tightly around myself. *On the pink chaise longue I sat down and wept*; ridiculous, I thought, crying anyway.

Michael returned carrying two teacups, one filled with whiskey, another with tea. "I didn't know which you'd prefer."

I'd just turned twenty-five. From this distance, it seems fitting—narratively cohesive—that modelling should taper off after Betty's death.

But I stopped modelling, in the end, abruptly. There came a morning I could barely rise from bed, and once upright, could not bend. Four injured discs, which could not be blamed solely on modelling: a typical complaint of the reluctantly tall, not helped by years writing in ergonomically compromising arrangements, folded in at a tiny 1930s sewing table, once my mother's.

There are very few sketches I kept, and those I did are bundled together in a drawer of Betty's old bureau, stashed away in a city I've not lived in for several years. There's only one I remember clearly: a four-hour charcoal drawing of me leaning against a mantelpiece, weight borne foolishly on one foot. The most excruciating pose I'd ever had the stubborn pride to withstand.

After the session, the artist had rolled up the drawing and handed it to me indifferently.

"Beauty bores me," she explained plainly, no trace of spite.

She herself was striking, merciless cheekbones and purposeful brown hands like Ricky Swallow carvings made animate.

What she may have meant was, Youth bores me. A sentiment I can hardly fault her on; who doesn't prefer a lived-in face?

The image, as I remember it, betrays nothing of those hours' discomfort. But although the body has no precise memory for pain, I can still sound the approximation of that agony, what was needed to stay so still.

A decade on, the only comparable stillness seems born of momentum, and time is rarely uncompromised by the compulsion to fill it, to make something useful of it. I find it near impossible to be still for long stretches, geographically as well as physically. Even reading, I carry the book from room to room.

I'm finishing this in Rome, a city indivisible from my grandmother, one that she loved best. A card arrives in my second week, from Betty's lifelong friend, Joan; *She would be thrilled to bits to know you were there. (What are you looking forward to?)*

Winter is listing into spring. A rare snowfall, powder-fine, windblown as mica from the first cherry blossoms, mantling the shoulders of headless statues in the Borghese gardens.

Inside the Galleria Borghese, Pluto's fingers press impossibly into Proserpina's thigh—the apotheosis of sculptural verisimilitude. Lower down, within casual arm's reach, Pluto's tendinous left calf, Proserpina's right ankle, and the intimately creased sole of her foot have been irreversibly discolored through centuries of the human impulse to touch marble coaxed to flesh.

Some evenings, passing through a central piazza at the winding down of tourist hours, I'll catch a street performer casting off the carapace of bronzed or gesso-stiff clothing, gathering up a skein of tulle after a day posing motionless in the guise of a famous statue. End-of-shift Berninis and Canovas, limbs and faces still dusted to effect stone: life imitating art imitating life.

JENNI FAGAN is an award-winning poet, novelist, and screenwriter who has written for the *New York Times,* the *Independent,* and *Marie Claire.* She was named a Scottish Author of the Year by the *Sunday Herald* and one of *Granta*'s Best of Young British Novelists, and has been short-listed for the International Impac Dublin Literary Award, the Sunday Times Short Story Award, and the BBC Short Story Award. She has completed the screenplay of her debut novel, *The Panopticon,* for Sixteen Films. Her directorial debut includes a short film made on the location that inspired the poem "Bangour Village Hospital (or) Edinburgh District Asylum." Fagan's work has been translated into eight languages.

Bangour Village Hospital (or) Edinburgh District Asylum

JENNI FAGAN

I was born here,
then a little while later I died.

Being born was something to do,
dying was something to do,

it was important—
to have something to do here.

After all these years.
After, all the lives I've lived!

Now I want to come back—
but they won't let me in.

We were refugees from reality.
Life escapees.

We knew what the worst thing was
so deeply in our bones

there could never
be any unknowing it.

They put a church in here.
There was a bell.

It tolled.
There was a holy man.

There was a shop.

There were green things in the outside world
and going there was helpful

but not beyond the end of the road.
Beyond the end of the road

there was judgement
and fear and anger.

People came from there,
wearing neat uniforms.

Everybody knew it.

Some of them had a kind hand.
Three did actually.

Three had a kind hand but they also had an unkind hand and those two
    hands often fought with each other—inside my body.

We had to be patient.
This was not a kind of dying.

Dying held no kindness
and we were labelled for patience.

They electrocuted
synaptic transmissions until we were all

forget-me-nots!
This was no metaphorical Sheol.

The church bell tolled
so the devil would know we were on to him

but he was so far down,
all the way down in my stomach like an apple pip

and I was born with that seed
my veins as branches—

like that it began to grow.

In 1906, it was 1906, in 1906
post came to the Edinburgh District Asylum.

There were people here for years before .
but nobody says it.

Two years before that the builders had left
clean worktops and sink taps

that could be turned
and water would come out

and it was hot or it was cold
but never both, the first ones turned

those taps so the rest of us could too.
They were the first ones.

They had no files.
Two years without an address,

it's not a place before a name
only a collection of walls

and scents, mostly Formica.
All of us were nameless.

Sometimes we shared a name
passed it around the wards at night

on a slip of sweetie wrapper,
pressed it into each other's hands

when the nurses weren't looking.
We swallowed that name

with our tablets, each would fall
through emptiness

and land with an echo
at the bottom

of Bangour Village Hospital's well.
Things swam down there.

Things so terrible
I have never been able to shine

a torch, but the others did
which is why they didn't make it.

I was always being born
and dying

and being born again.
I decided to stop being born.

I decided to wear ugliness like fine silk pyjamas.

I'd just be in this skin
even if I never wanted it in the first place.

Who could be so ungrateful?
Uncertain bones still walk—some.

So it was we were given wreaths
to wear in our hair,

made of hope and true heart
but often laced with spiritual squalor

we decorated them with daisies
and we never fed the botanist who muttered

only about weeds. In 1918
they brought in normal people to a new general hospital on our grounds.

We knew they were normal
because they told us so. They told each other too.

They had meetings in case
anyone was uncertain.

Just to be sure who was what,
it's good to be sure about these things.

We were us and they were them.
We were the others but *they* were unlovable to us!

They modelled Bangour on Alt-Scherbitz.
Do you know it?

We were an asylum of village psychiatric.
Not village people.

One doctor played a harp
and sang about the preservation society.

There was a holy, holy workshop, a holy recreation hall,
it smelled like school-murk, dink-dank.

Each villa held thirty.
There were chickens.

They called that patch a farm.
It did grow onions and also potatoes.

All faiths were welcome in the church but some were more welcome than
     others.

We had incinerators.
We had a railway connection.

We had a library.
The railway line left this place, it was cyclical as rebirth and decay.

They let us in here between the wars.
Then after 1945 we took it back for a good, long time.

We were crazy in a village in the eighties.
Your fashion was awful.

Our architect was Hippolyte Blanc.

He put an Edwardian Baroque hall at the centre of thirteen (it couldn't be
     twelve seeing as we were not a whole set of seasons) and the church
     was Romanesque, the latter belonging to H. O. Tarbolton.

Nobody called him Ho, in public.

Our railway did not take us to the world beyond the tracks.

It was authorised by the Edinburgh and District Lunacy Board
to run one way only.

It brought coal and tablets, mountains of tablets
as big as the mountains of coal

and neat plastic fetishised needles
and fresh electric probes

and one day riding high on that train an electric machine to shock us all.
But machines in themselves

are not shocking.
It's the kind of people

who design them—
say one little boy pulls on a cat's tail,

drags it into the bush
tells his audience

see what will happen when I cut out its brain
with a scalpel?

They shut the railway soon after.
Even things coming in one way was a direction too many.

Static were the trees.
Static were the stones.

The house of God Stands Open to Thee Forever—
until it does not of course.

Some people were happy here
with trees of evil in their Gutula.

It was a place to come.
You can see that, can't you?

When rooms were unsafe
and street corners worse

there was always here to come and stand and know the trees and the
dark and the wards and the meds and the fear and the strange and the
faces old and new.

Now where is there?

One day they moved a wooden
building lest we think it were a fixed thing.

Now out there in the community it is all waiting lists.
Often not even places of bricks to go to.

Nothing.
Just a street corner.

Where is there now?

566 of ours had unmarked graves
right on this site.

Not on the cricket ground.
You can walk there but don't think we can't see you.

Lights out is coming again, in the end.
We all knew it would.

Lights out. Lights out.
Can you hear the bell?

Our dreams had dates with nightmares.
They took over the grounds until dawn.

We were not the war veterans who spent time here
broken but so brave

we were something to fear
or hide

or deny
we were always low on tobacco and Largactil.

We know soldiers roamed
those grounds at night

and all that was left of them
were hankies.

There were good nurses
and there were bad nurses,

so says every family.

Some went.
They all went.

But, many came back again and again.
We never left Ward 9 unmanned—

some feedback
you see

is best delivered from the grave.

You can't medicate a spirit.
You can't pinch it,

or electrocute it,
or drop water on its brain.

Most especially you can't heal it.
We were so beyond all that.

We bided our time.
Those who died moved into Ward 9 so we would know they'd never
      leave us.

All the nurses were too scared to go in the patients' lift.

We still had hearts
and they were beating

but when all that stopped
we'd join Ward 9.

It was somewhere to go.
Having somewhere to go was important.

The voices nurses heard were not ours
and they knew it

and we all knew collectively that one day only birds would live here.
In these empty wards.

Each bird chirping.
Nesting.

Little bird-babies with gilded golden cages
around their black hearts.

They give us no silence.

DAVID MITCHELL is the award-winning and bestselling author of *The Bone Clocks*, *The Thousand Autumns of Jacob de Zoet*, *Black Swan Green*, *Cloud Atlas*, *Number9Dream*, and *Ghostwritten*. Twice short-listed for the Man Booker Prize, Mitchell was named one of the hundred most influential people in the world by *Time* magazine in 2007. With his wife, KA Yoshida, Mitchell co-translated the international bestselling memoir *The Reason I Jump* from the Japanese. His latest novel, *Slade House*, was published in October 2015. He lives in Ireland with his wife and two children.

Repeats

DAVID MITCHELL

M y oh my, two visitors in one hour. I feel like the Godfather, holding court, in that scene at the beginning. What's that? Speak up, I'm virtually deaf, these days. Who? My last visitor? Oh, him. He only left a few minutes ago. You passed each other in the Garden of Remembrance, in all likelihood. You wouldn't have recognised him. I rather fear, if I gave you the full story, you'd think, *Poor old boy, he's lost the plot completely.* There again, where's the fun in being dead by Sunday if I can't misplace a plot or two? I'll tell you the story if you want to hear it. Let me set the scene first. Old habits die hard. Otherwise they wouldn't be old habits, would they?

All my life, a man, a particular man, has been watching me. I spotted him only on rare occasions. Only when the light was just so. Only when I was seeing and not just looking. Or should that be 'looking and not just seeing'? You're the wordsmith of the family, not me. What were we talking about? Oh, yes, the watcher. Stop interrupting. It's distracting. So the first time was at my seventh birthday party. I was given a board game called Pit Stop. Dead simple—this was before smartphones, before any of these gizmos—but gosh, I loved that game. You threw the dice and moved your little racing car round and round the fold-out track, skidding on oil spills, getting waylaid in the pit or wedged in by other players. There was me, Dean

Moran, Jason Taylor and Neil Brose, playing on the kitchen table in the wreckage of my birthday tea. I can see the picture as clearly as yesterday. Actually, a lot *more* clearly than yesterday. Mid-game, I looked up and there he was, at the window. An old man in a funeral suit, a snazzy hat—a fedora, if you're interested—and those black shiny sunglasses favoured by FBI agents. FBI agents in the movies, at least. Watching us. Watching me. Not menacingly; just attentively. I assumed he was the grandfather of one of my guests, so I asked my playmates who he was. Jason Taylor asked who I meant. I pointed, but there was nobody there. Neil Brose handed me the dice. 'Your turn.' I returned to Pit Stop. A child is one who is unshackled by the need for logical explanations.

The next time, I was ten years old. It was a school day, but I was at home, convalescing from the mumps. The mumps jab hadn't been invented yet. Mum warned me not to watch TV all day and went off to work. I watched TV all day. *The Invisible Man* was on, I remember. Ring any bells? No? *The Invisible Man* starred David McCallum as a scientist whose experiment goes wrong and leaves him totally see-through. He soon learns that invisibility is perhaps the crappiest of superpowers, unless you're a confirmed nudist. Think about it. Luckily, David McCallum also invents a skin-coloured latex paint and has a good line in floppy golden wigs. This lets him dress up as himself when he wants to mingle with others; and unpeel his epidermal layer to pass undetected and spy on the bad guys. The show was a repeat. An alien concept to your generation, I know. Repeats were simply TV programmes that had been aired before. Back in those days, you see, there was a grand total of three TV channels. Yes. Three in total, and they were only on between about 9 a.m. and midnight—but there *still* weren't enough programmes to fill even those limited broadcasting hours. Repeats or nothing. That was the choice. What were we saying?

240

Yes yes yes. That day, midway through *The Invisible Man*, I saw him again. The old man. The Watcher. Same suit, same hat, same sunglasses. Not standing outside the window this time, but in the corner. Just watching. Was I scared? Not exactly. 'Scared' is too blunt a word. Most emotions are knots of several threads, pulled tight. The Watcher was a watcher. Not a murderer, not a threat, not an interventionist. He had no corporeal presence . . . but he wasn't an evil spirit, either. How did I know? Like how you know a dog isn't going to bite. Call it instinct, call it what you will; you just know. I asked him if I was imagining him. Behind his glasses, the Watcher did that face you do when a kid asks you a super-perceptive question you'd need all day to answer, but alas you don't have all day. Something thumped against the window. A bird, possibly. When I looked back, the Watcher was gone.

No, I told not a soul. I may have been only ten years of age, but even I knew that confessing to being spied upon by a snazzily dressed senior citizen who flitted into and out of reality was not a clever move. My adolescence came and went, but still I felt no need to 'explain' the Watcher to myself. Lots of things in the world we don't understand. Endocrinology. Airline ticket pricing. Spousal intentions. Life trundles on regardless. The Watcher was just an occasional blip in my otherwise normal existence. Very occasional, very normal. Didn't see him again until my first year at college. I'd spent a night with a girl. My first time. She was in the shower, washing me off her skin. I was blowing her Native American dreamcatcher to make it spin, thinking about . . . God knows what. 'Friday I'm in Love' by the Cure on her record player. I remember that. The girl was a big, hairy goth. The needle got stuck on the same bit. I sat up to fix it, and there he was, watching me from her dressing table in the corner of the room. That time, I admit, I made a shocked noise like GAH! 'What is it?' The goth in the shower was now the goth at the door. I blurted out I'd had a nightmare about being chased by a grass snake as big as a train. My fib got her more turned on than my fledgling skills as a Casanova, if I'm honest. She was a psychology undergraduate.

The Earth revolved on its axis. The Earth spun around our sun. Do you ever feel that you're caught in a spiral? Or that you *are* the spiral, and that what we call 'right now' is the tip of a stylus, travelling round and around? I did the things people do. I made a little money, I watched youth slip away, I found a partner. I saw the Watcher twice, three times perhaps, per decade. When I cut your umbilical cord, he was at the gynaecologist's side, watching. When I buried your grandfather, he shared the vicar's umbrella. After your mother and I got divorced, he dropped by. That was a significant visit. Do you remember that old flat, down by the station? Quite the shit-hole. The noise of revelry and fights would wash up from the Railway Pub and in through the window . . . I steeped myself in the nastiness of the place for a year, as a penance. One night—one dusk, in midsummer—I couldn't sleep, and I had *The Invisible Man* on, on YouTube. There he was. Not standing, this time, but sitting, in the other armchair. Watching. This time I spoke to him. Told him how my life hadn't turned out as I'd hoped. He didn't judge me. A thought occurred to me, and I asked him not to go yet. I went to the hallway, returned with my fedora and FBI sunglasses and sat back down opposite him. We mirrored each other, until he took his shades and hat off. Upon seeing his face for the first time, I realised I'd always known who he was. I just hadn't known I'd known. Like all the most important stuff, right?

You can guess who. The menu at the Twist in the Tale Cafe is not long. The Watcher was twenty years older than me—I was fifty by then, and he looked about seventy—but there was no doubt that he was me. We didn't speak. He knew what I knew: and what he knew that I didn't know, I preferred not to ask. Tiredness dragged me under, eventually. That divorce will be miserable and costly, you can predict; nobody warns you how exhausting it is. Didn't wake until the stars were out. He was gone. Moths clustered on my laptop. Some itch no longer itched, and the Watcher didn't visit again until today. He sat where you're sitting. He spoke in my croaky husk. 'You look worse than I do.' I gave him a skinny, bony finger. He said, 'Would you care to watch a film with me?'

I told him the hospice already had Netflix.

He explained that he meant the film of our life.

I asked if it was true, then. You get to see it all.

He told me that yes, it's true, you do, if you want to.

So I asked him if the film of my life was worth watching.

The film of *our* life, he corrected me, is a mixed bag. Chances are seized, chances get frittered. The family stuff's nice, looking back. The sex scenes are nothing to get excited about, but the parts where I act so damn sure I know what's going on are comedy gold. He spoke about a watcher's perspective. How life is lived strapped to itself, like Odysseus bound to the mast. But a watcher has time to discern patterns; patterns in the patterns; patterns begetting patterns. He was going to watch the whole thing again. From the very first frame, in real time. He invited me to join him. I hesitated. He knew why, and warned me that the famous white light you float towards at the moment of death is, in fact, the afterimage of the bulb on the darkness. Beyond lay an eternity of nothing. That's the choice. Repeats or nothing.

Do you ever feel that you're caught in a spiral? Or that you are the spiral? Three visitors in one hour. I feel like the Godfather. You'll have to speak up I'm afraid. I'm virtually deaf. You passed my last two visitors in the Garden of Remembrance, chances are. They were together. If I gave you the full story, you'd think, Poor old boy, he's lost the plot completely. There again, where's the fun in being dead by Sunday if I can't misplace plots? All my life, two men, two particular men, have been watching me. I spotted them only on rare occasions. Only when the light was just so.

DEBORAH LANDAU is the author of three collections of poetry, most recently *The Uses of the Body*. She directs the Creative Writing Program at New York University. Her fourth book, *Soft Targets*, is forthcoming from Copper Canyon Press in 2019.

When It Comes to This Fleshed Neck

DEBORAH LANDAU

When it comes to this fleshed neck
even a finger could do it,

even a sharp stick,
a blunt blow, a fall—

my jugular,
there's a soft target.

and night is a soft target,
all of us within it,

Osama shot dead
in his pajamas

And everyone
on the Brooklyn-bound F

as the man removes a bomb
from his bag—

a square of chocolate
he detonates in his mouth

KANAKO NISHI was born in Tehran in 1977, and grew up in Cairo and Osaka. She made her debut as a writer in 2004 with *Aoi* (Blue). In 2007, her novel *Tsutenkaku* (Tower to heaven) won the Sakunosuke Oda Prize. In 2012 she received the first Hayao Kawai Prize for her novel *Fukuwarai* (Funny face). Her masterpiece, *Saraba!* won the prestigious Naoki Prize in 2015. She lives in Tokyo.

ALLISON MARKIN POWELL is a literary translator, editor, and publishing consultant in New York City. Her translation of Hiromi Kawakami's *Strange Weather in Tokyo* (originally published as *The Briefcase*) was nominated for the Man Asian Literary Prize and the Independent Foreign Fiction Prize. Her other translations include works by Osamu Dazai, Fuminori Nakamura, and Kaho Nakayama. She maintains the database Japanese Literature in English.

Burn

KANAKO NISHI
TRANSLATED FROM THE JAPANESE
BY ALLISON MARKIN POWELL

I had always worn pants.

I hated those cutesy pants for girls with ribbon designs or frills on the hem. The pants I wanted to wear—and actually ended up wearing—were hand-me-downs from my two much older brothers. My favorites were a pair of worn-out cutoff jean shorts from my oldest brother (these were very rock-and-roll) and a pair of track pants with a white double stripe down the sides from my middle brother (these were very hip-hop).

My mom would smile when she saw me wearing these, but my grandma who lived with us always made a disgusted face (she really did look disgusted—it was the perfect fusion of dislike and disappointment, as if a complete stranger had suddenly presented her with a gift of cow manure).

"You're a girl, Kei, you should dress more like one."

Grandma said this to me only when it was just the two of us. We would be in her room, which was Japanese-style and just off the living room. It got magnificent sunlight and always carried the sweet scent of freshly cut peaches, but Grandma hated this room.

"I don't want people to think just because I'm old I like tatami mats."

Grandma was always quite stylish. She'd wear a light purple dress embellished with pretty lace on the bodice, or a formfitting skirt the color of sunset, her nails perfectly manicured, and even just in the house she'd have on large earrings. She never wore pants, no matter how cold it was, and of course boyish things like what I wore were out of the question.

Mom was totally different from Grandma. She always wore baggy jeans held up sloppily with a belt. She cut her hair short, and in contrast to Grandma's impeccable grooming, I can't even remember seeing her wear lipstick. She'd sip her coffee while smoking a cigarette, and when she laughed, she opened her mouth so wide you could see all of her molars. It almost seemed as though my mother had made flippancy her mission.

My desire to dress like a boy absolutely delighted my mother, yet whenever my older brothers did anything that was the slightest bit "macho" (Mom used the English word), she would make a disgusted face. This was exactly the same expression that Grandma showed me. As if a complete stranger had suddenly presented her with a gift of cow manure—*that* face.

"From now on, I don't care whether you're a boy or a girl. Girlish, boyish—it's all ridiculous, isn't it!"

Mom and Grandma were such complete opposites. They ate dinner together every night, but the two of them hardly ever looked each other in the eye and had a conversation. My father wasn't around. He left home before I even started crawling. Mom had gotten rid of every last photograph of him, so I didn't know what he looked like, and I never asked her or Grandma about him.

Grandma pleaded, "At least let her hair grow," so Mom left my hair long. That was the only girlish thing about me. Here was a point that even Mom seemed to concede, however reluctantly. My hair represented neutral ground between her and Grandma.

And so my hair grew down to my shoulder blades, and was always tied up carelessly. I even made it look messier on purpose. One time when I took a bath, a dead insect fell from the tangles of my hair, and Mom clapped her hands in laughter.

I always played with the boys. And among them, I was the boss. I refused to tolerate anyone claiming a position of superiority over me. I was tall and long-limbed. Nobody could throw the dodgeball farther or climb a higher tree. I was the one who came up with the cruelest way to kill butterflies (bury their wings in the sand and crush their bodies with the seesaw), and it was also me who came up with the most scathing name—"McShit!"— for the crazy old man we liked to cuss out (I had no idea what it meant but it still gave me satisfying goose bumps to say it).

The boys followed behind me, awaiting my command. When occasionally some kid would tug on my "girlish" long hair, the rest of them would beat on him until he started crying. Whenever Mom saw me leading the boys around, she couldn't help laughing out loud.

When I was in fifth grade, Grandma went into the hospital. At first it was just for tests. Grandma had been looking thin ever since complaining to me about vague stomach pains, but after they decided to fully admit her, she seemed to wither away before our eyes, like a wilting vegetable.

Mom and I went to the hospital every day. Sometimes one or the other of my brothers came with us, but they never stayed for long. My oldest brother was obsessed with rugby, and my middle brother was crazy about baseball. Of course, Mom made her disgusted face at both of them.

Grandma would have on lipstick even in her hospital room. She kept a pouch filled with all kinds of makeup beside the bed, and that same sweet scent hung in the room. Since her earlobes had grown too thin to hold her clip-on earrings, she said she wanted to get her ears pierced, but Mom wouldn't hear of it. So Grandma started wearing the earrings that wouldn't stay on her ears as pendants around her neck.

Around the same time that Grandma went into the hospital, my breasts suddenly began to grow. It really happened all of a sudden. My breasts hurt and there was nothing I could do about it—plus I was embarrassed because the other girls were still flat as boards. The rest of my body grew round, just like my breasts. The sleeves of the boys' T-shirts I wore clung tightly to my arms, and when I wore shorts there was something suggestive about my thighs.

This was around the time when people started telling me I was pretty. At first it was the ladies in the neighborhood. "Oh, Kei, how pretty you've gotten!" they would say.

After a while I realized that what their compliments were describing was not my childishness. This coincided with a gradual shift in the way my classmates treated me as well. The girls would gather around, asking if they could touch my hair, and without asking they would comb it with their pink and purple glitter brushes. And I would catch the boys staring at me all the time. Whenever our eyes met, the boy would look away, embarrassed. This happened even with the boy who had been beaten so harshly for pulling my hair.

"Maybe I should wear a skirt."

Mom just stared back at me when I suggested this one day. She seemed defensive, but she did not make her disgusted face.

"I'd like to wear it for Grandma, you know?"

I decided on a simple, navy blue skirt. Of course, I would have been embarrassed to wear something that was too girly.

Still, when we saw Grandma in the hospital, she was completely thrilled. She hugged me with her twig-like arms (she was shockingly frail), and brushed my hair until she fell asleep, exhausted from the effort. My hair, amber colored and gleaming from being brushed every day, now smelled of Grandma's sweet scent. This made the girls in my class all the more obsessed with it.

Despite the skirt's simplicity, once I put it on, the boys' T-shirts no longer suited me. But when I tried on a blouse that went with the skirt, my breasts showed through, so I had to wear a sports bra. I was self-conscious about anyone seeing the straps, so I left my hair loose over my shoulders.

Now, no matter how you looked at me, I was obviously a girl.

Grandma was all smiles in her hospital room (as if she had never shown me her disgusted face). She grew even thinner, and Mom's conversations with the doctor made the bags under her eyes darker by the day, but I took pride in the happiness that Grandma seemed to derive from seeing me.

"How pretty you look!"

Sometimes Grandma mistakenly called me by my mother's name.

"Maki, you really are pretty!"

At my school's field day that year, I didn't finish in first place in the footrace, for the first time.

"How pretty."

That's what the man said when I encountered him. I was on my way home from school.

I still don't know why I was walking alone on that street along the housing complex—it wasn't the way I usually went.

"You got second place in the dash, didn't you?"

He called the footrace a dash. Something about the way he said it sounded childlike to me, even though I was the child and he was definitely the adult. The light was behind him so I couldn't really see his face, but he was tall with a bald head and a scraggly beard. It was as if his face would materialize only when he swiveled his head around.

"How pretty."

When I got home that day, Mom took one look at my skirt and called the police.

She stripped me naked and examined every inch of my body, then scrubbed me as vigorously as if I were a burdock root. The man's "stuff" (this was what Mom called it) was smeared on my skirt like some kind of sign or portent.

As Mom washed me roughly, every so often she cried out.

"You see!"

I didn't say a word, I just let Mom do what she was doing to me. I couldn't bring myself to say, *Don't rub me so hard, it hurts*. My skin tingled for days afterward.

At school they held a full assembly. My mother was not the kind of person to keep quiet about what had happened to me. The principal used the phrase "a student at our school," but in no time at all, everyone seemed to know that it was me he was talking about. In the midst of their shouting about the creepy guy who had been at our field day and about the fact that there was a crazy guy lurking around the housing complex, everyone tried to console me.

"Poor Kei!"

The man was never arrested.

I went back to wearing pants. Mom told me to.

"I don't want you giving them any strange ideas."

We threw away that skirt. Or rather, it was set on fire. Mom burned it along with other garbage in the yard.

I didn't wear my brothers' hand-me-down pants anymore. Mom burned the rock-and-roll jeans and the hip-hop track pants too. My oldest brother had left home and moved into a dorm in order to focus on rugby, and my middle brother had quit baseball, dyed his hair blond, and hardly ever came home. Mom started burning everything they had left behind.

"If they left it here, that means they don't need it!"

Mom became obsessed with the act of burning things. She was completely fixated on setting aflame anything we didn't need.

Every day, when I came home from school, I could see smoke rising from the yard. This was the evidence of my mother's anger. She had been angry ever since that day. Terribly angry, all the time. Whether it was about what had happened to me, or about the man not being arrested—more than either of these, Mom just seemed angry about everything.

"You see!"

One day I looked in the yard to see Mom burning Grandma's clothes—Grandma who was, by the way, still alive. There were fewer and fewer things inside our house.

But my closet was stocked with new pants. Heavy denim jeans and khaki cargo pants. Grandma didn't know about what had happened to me. By that time, when we would visit her hospital room, Grandma barely even knew who I was anymore.

I started watching the old man out back because of Mom's "burning things" phase. I'm sure none of the other students in the classroom were unnerved by the smoke rising outside the window during our lessons. Tracing the source of the smoke, I saw the janitor, who was burning something in the incinerator.

Nobody knew the old man's name. The students all called him "the old man out back"—really he seemed quite ancient.

The old man out back was generally to be found in the courtyard (who knows why we referred to it as "out back"). He tended the flower beds and he must have been the one who took care of the school's rabbits, but he was most often at the incinerator. Printouts and wooden chairs that were no longer in use, long-unclaimed lost clothing and fallen leaves, dried-out and rotting gourd vines. The old man burned anything. I wondered why I had never noticed the smoke until now, though it easily drifted up past our third-story classroom.

Now my eye was constantly drawn to the figure of the old man. Fortunately my seat was by the window. Neither the teacher nor the students reproached me for being so distracted in class. After all, I was the "poor thing." It was quiet for me within those quotation marks, and as long as I stayed there, I was safe. Aside from giving me sympathetic looks, everyone pretty much left me alone. There was enormous power within those quotation marks.

There were times when I felt as though I myself were encased in glass. It may sound like a totally predictable way to describe it, but so what—that's how it really was. Everyone's voice sounded distant, like when you're underwater. Whenever I caught anyone's eyes—boys or girls—they all had their own way of averting their gaze. The boys usually turned red in the face.

I had grown quite thin. Yet my breasts had not gotten any smaller. I looked much more grown-up compared with the other girls my age.

And every day I watched the old man from the window.

He was always burning something. He burned all sorts of items—I was often impressed by the sheer number of things he found to burn.

I became obsessed with the old man's craftiness. *Oh, that's too much—there's no way that's going to burn*, I would think to myself about something or other, but in the old man's hands, it just went up in smoke.

Speaking of burning things, my mom was doing exactly the same thing, and yet it seemed different from what the old man did. If Mom seemed to be burning things as punishment for something, the old man out back's way of burning things seemed more like consolation.

The incinerator looked like a monster with a huge mouth. The old man had tamed the monster—he was like a wild-animal trainer, gently offering a sacrifice.

After a while it wasn't enough just to watch from above, so one day I went down into the courtyard. I sat on the raised flower bed that was behind the incinerator, and silently gazed at the old man.

That's not to say that I spoke to him. I didn't say a word—I was perfectly satisfied just to watch as he went about what he was doing.

The old man didn't look at me. Sometimes he would sit in a folding chair that was left nearby and smoke a cigarette (the old man used the incinerator to light his cigarettes too—I always held my breath, hoping that he wouldn't burn himself as he brought his cigarette close to the incinerator, but like magic, he always found a little flame), though even then, he still didn't look at me.

He was the first person who didn't even try to look at me.

All the others—even when they ultimately averted their gaze—looked at me at least once. There were adults who gawked in wide-eyed astonishment, girls who smiled gently at me, and boys who stared with moist eyes. But the old man didn't look at me.

I doubted that he hadn't noticed me. Occasionally I coughed from the smoke, or the afternoon sun cast my shadow over his feet.

It seemed to me that the old man's not looking at me was different from the way other grown-up men behaved. Ever since the incident, grown-up men no longer spoke to elementary school girls. The guy still hadn't been caught, and so perhaps they couldn't bear the idea of being called out for staring at a girl for just a moment too long. If any adult man looked at us, he would then run off.

But I had the feeling that this wasn't the reason why the old man didn't look at me. Even though we hadn't yet said a word to each other, I was almost certain he wasn't that kind of coward.

That's why I wasn't surprised when finally one day, the old man out back spoke to me.

"Is there something you would like to burn?"

He still didn't look at me when he said this, but there was no doubt he was talking to me. Besides the two of us, there was no one else in the courtyard. At that point, I was brazenly leaving the classroom in the middle of a lesson. If I said I wasn't feeling well, the teacher simply gave me permission to go to the nurse's office, even knowing that I would soon be in the courtyard without having gone to the nurse—nobody gave me a hard time. I don't know if the teachers ever said anything to the other students, but since I did this on my own, I figured there wasn't any harm in it.

"To burn?" I asked.

"Yes, is there something you would like to burn?" the old man repeated politely.

I was glad he didn't say anything to me about being out of class, and I was even more grateful that he didn't try to make stupid small talk about the weather. The old man was clearly asking whether I had any business to take care of. I felt like he was treating me as if I was an adult, and I appreciated being addressed so politely.

"Something I would like to burn?"

"Yes."

The old man was brusque. And yet his brusqueness did not make me feel isolated. I shoved my hand in my pocket and pulled out a crumpled wad of tissue about the size of a walnut. I was embarrassed by how tiny it was, but the old man nodded briefly, which gave me courage.

"I see, there you have it."

At that moment, I saw the old man's face clearly for the first time. His eyes were big. Goggle-eyed was the perfect description, but not in a scary way at all. There were deep wrinkles all over the old man's face.

Carefully, he put the bit of tissue into the incinerator. Even though it was so small, he didn't just toss it in. I doubt there has ever been a piece of tissue that has been burned so conscientiously.

From then on, the old man would burn something for me every day.

A roll left over from lunchtime (I was glad he didn't tell me I was being wasteful), a mess-up from calligraphy class (the characters for "friend"), a broken hair-elastic (found in the bottom of my school satchel). The old man never once made fun of me. Whenever I showed up, he always asked me as if for the first time: "Is there something you would like to burn?"

Not once did he crack a joke or say something like, "You again?" When it came to burning things, the old man was a professional.

It didn't matter whether or not he knew anything about the incident. What was important was that the old man didn't put me into the quotation marks of being the "poor thing." He simply treated me with respect, as someone who brought him things to burn each day. And I was courteous to him in return. I didn't make pointless conversation, nor did I try to ingratiate myself by predicting what would or wouldn't burn. As far as burning things was concerned, it was best to leave it up to the old man.

"Is there something you would like to burn?"

It rained for the first time since I had been going to see the old man out back.

Of course, that didn't stop him from burning things. Wearing a black rain poncho, he made sure the incinerator's flame didn't go out.

I carried an umbrella. I had thought that rain ponchos were only for little kids, but the old man wore his quite well. Holding my umbrella, I felt timid and childlike (even though I actually was a child).

"Is there something you would like to burn?"

I had shown up that day without anything to burn. Perhaps it was the rain that had eased my tension.

I expected it to be all right to show up empty-handed. Nevertheless, at the time, I still felt self-conscious about being there without anything to burn. It seemed like a rather rude way to behave toward a professional like the old man.

"I'm sorry."

The old man just stared at me when I apologized. His face really was etched with wrinkles.

"I don't have anything to burn."

"I see."

The old man's gaze remained fixed on me. It had been a long while since an adult had looked at me for such a sustained amount of time.

"Please don't apologize," the old man said. "There's no need to burn things just for the sake of burning them, is there?"

The old man spun around and returned to his work. He was so intent on his burning, it was as though I had not been there in the first place.

Raindrops were falling on the old man's hood, and on my little umbrella as well.

The patter of the rain as it hit my umbrella, and then the ground, had gradually grown louder.

"What about words?"

The old man paused in his task when I said this. I wanted him to look at me some more. I wanted him to see me more clearly. My wish was granted. Slowly the old man turned back around.

"Can you burn words?"

The old man thought about this for a moment. There was nothing mystified or scornful in his expression, and to be sure, he did not make any sort of disgusted face.

"Burn words, you say?"

"Yes. Can you burn words?"

I didn't wait for the old man to reply. Before he could say anything, I spat out, "You see!"

Just then I felt a chill between my legs. It wasn't because of the rain. Despite the downpour, it was quite warm by the incinerator.

"Can you burn the words, 'You see'? I was wearing a skirt. But then there was a strange man. He told me I was pretty. And that's what my mother said."

I got that far and then fell silent. I didn't think it was fair to talk about my mom, and if I said any more I was likely to burst into tears.

"Unfortunately you cannot burn words," the old man said. Raindrops were trickling from the brim of his hood. "You cannot burn things that don't have any shape."

The old man looked even more regretful than me. It was as though he was even more distressed, and always had been, by the fact that you couldn't burn things that don't have any shape.

"I understand," I said.

Shrouded by the rain and smoke, the old man's figure was limply distorted.

"I'm very sorry"—he coughed as he spoke—"that I'm not able to burn the thing you very much want to burn."

His response to my question brought him just slightly outside the realm of his professionalism, although he was still second to none in his conversational restraint and his lack of banter.

"The thing I very much want to burn."

I was sweating. From the tip of my nose, under my arms, in my crotch.

"Yes. I'm sorry I can't be of assistance."

I couldn't stop sweating. I was thinking of Mom. Of her sending up angry smoke signals as she burned everything.

"My mother . . ."

My heart was pounding, my bangs were soaking wet.

"She's sure it was my fault."

I was clutching Mom's "You see!" tightly within my hand. It may not have had any shape but it was ice cold, and it made my palm shiver slightly.

You see.

I understood. I knew what Mom meant when she said that.

I had used the excuse that I wanted to show Grandma, but the truth was, I had wanted to be pretty. I had wanted to wear a skirt.

I had thought it was cute, and I was happy when everyone else thought I looked pretty.

You see.

I knew that what happened that day had been payback for taking pleasure in being told I was pretty, for going against Mom's wishes and being girlish. And that it was my fault my cute skirt had been stained with the man's whatever-it-was. It was all because of me.

"It was my fault."

It was embarrassing to talk about this with the old man. I wanted him to remain professional. More than for myself, I just wanted him to be out here with the flames. And yet, I couldn't help wanting him to look at me.

"It wasn't your fault," the old man said.

His voice had never sounded so dry. Dry, forceful, and warm. Just like the flames themselves. And undaunted by the rain, of course.

"It was not your fault."

There was something running from my eyes, but it definitely wasn't tears. Somehow, they didn't deserve to be called tears. Whatever it was, they were stickier than tears, and gave off a strong smell. And anyway, I certainly wasn't crying.

"But I . . ."

I wanted to wear a skirt. The skirt was cute. I looked pretty wearing the skirt. I liked that people thought I was pretty. And then, look what happened. That man said I was pretty. And I even liked that too. It made me happy. I was happy to be told I was pretty. But I . . .

"It wasn't your fault."

It wasn't my fault.

There was nothing wrong with wanting to be pretty. There was nothing wrong with being happy when somebody said I was pretty.

There was nothing wrong with being pretty.

"It was not your fault. Absolutely not. Do you understand?"

"Yes."

260

The truth was, I didn't really understand. How could the old man declare it with such certainty? How could he know "absolutely"? But his words gave me warmth. That's what was important.

"It wasn't my fault."

As I said this, even the palm of my hand felt warm. The words "You see!" probably hadn't disappeared—they would always be there—but they no longer made me shiver.

The old man coughed once more and then he turned his back again.

I could tell, just from his back, that the old man felt ashamed. Even just the few words that made up our conversation—to the old man, it was unthinkably idle chatter.

As if to recover what was left, the old man earnestly set about burning things. A flattened red-and-white gym hat, a wooden plank of unimaginable use, a bumblebee that had died inside the box where the thermometer was kept.

I just sat and watched all this. It kept on raining, but I felt warm.

Because it wasn't my fault.

Grandma died that night.

Her body was cremated. As Mom watched the smoke rise, all of us were surprised by how loudly she wailed. I had never seen Mom cry before, and it was the first time I ever heard her call Grandma "Mama."

Contributor Notes

Eric Abrahamsen is a translator and promoter of Chinese fiction. His translation of Xu Zechen's *Running Through Beijing* was shortlisted for the National Translation Award, and his short story translations have appeared in magazines including the *New Yorker* and *Granta*. He runs the website Paper Republic, which introduces Chinese literature in translation, and also works as a literary agent and publishing consultant.

Julia Alvarez has written novels (*How the García Girls Lost Their Accents*, *In the Time of the Butterflies*, *Saving the World*, *In the Name of Salomé*, and *¡Yo!*), collections of poems (*Homecoming*, *The Other Side/El Otro Lado*, and *The Woman I Kept to Myself*), nonfiction (*Something to Declare*, *Once Upon a Quinceañera: Coming of Age in the USA*, and *A Wedding in Haiti*), and numerous books for young readers (including the *Tía Lola Stories* series, *Before We Were Free*, *finding miracles*, *Return to Sender*, and *Where Do They Go?*). A recipient of a 2013 National Medal of Arts, Alvarez is one of the founders of Border of Lights, a movement to promote peace and collaboration between Haiti and the Dominican Republic. She lives in Vermont.

Tahmima Anam was born in Dhaka, Bangladesh, and is the author of three novels: *A Golden Age*, which was awarded the Commonwealth Writers' Prize for Best First Book; *The Good Muslim*; and most recently, *The Bones of Grace*. In 2013 she was selected as one of *Granta*'s Best of Young British Novelists.

Margaret Atwood is the author of more than fifty books of fiction, poetry, and critical essays. Her recent novels are *The Heart Goes Last* and the MaddAddam trilogy: *Oryx and Crake* (shortlisted for the Giller and Man Booker prizes), *The Year of the Flood*, and *Madd-Addam*. Other novels include *The Blind Assassin*, winner of the Man Booker Prize; *Alias Grace*; *The Robber Bride*; *Cat's Eye*; *The Penelopiad*, a retelling of the *Odyssey*; and the modern classic *The Handmaid's Tale*, now a critically acclaimed television series. *Hag-Seed*, a novelistic revisitation of Shakespeare's play *The Tempest*, was published in 2016. Her most recent graphic series is *Angel Catbird*. In 2017, she was awarded the German Peace Prize, the Franz Kafka International Literary Prize, and the PEN Center USA Lifetime Achievement Award.

Eula Biss is the author, most recently, of *On Immunity: An Inoculation*, which was named one of the Ten Best Books of 2014 by the *New York Times Book Review*. Her second book, *Notes from No Man's Land: American Essays*, won the National Book Critics Circle Award for criticism in 2010. Her first book, *The Balloonists*, was published by Hanging Loose Press in 2002. Her writing has been supported by a Guggenheim Fellowship, a Howard Foundation Fellowship, an NEA Literature Fellowship, and a Rona Jaffe Writers' Award. She holds a BA in nonfiction writing from Hampshire College and an MFA. in nonfiction writing from the University of Iowa. Her essays have recently appeared in the *Believer*, *Harper's*, and the *New York Times Magazine*.

Lan Samantha Chang is the author of *Hunger: A Novella and Stories*, and two novels, *Inheritance* and *All Is Forgotten, Nothing Is*

Lost. Her work has been translated into nine languages and has been chosen twice for inclusion in *The Best American Short Stories*. She has received creative writing fellowships from Stanford University, the Radcliffe Institute for Advanced Study, the Guggenheim Foundation, and the National Endowment for the Arts.

Jaime Cortez is a writer and visual artist based in Northern California. His fiction, essays, and drawings have appeared in diverse publications that include *Kindergarde: Avant-Garde Poems, Plays, Stories, and Songs for Children* (2103, edited by Dana Teen Lomax for Black Radish Books); *No Straight Lines*, a forty-year compendium of LGBT comics (2012, edited by Justin Hall for Fantagraphics Books); *Street Art San Francisco: Mission Muralismo* (2009, edited by Annice Jacoby for Abrams Press); and *Infinite City*, an experimental atlas of San Francisco (2010, edited by Rebecca Solnit for University of California Press). Jaime is currently working on a short-story collection.

Linda Coverdale has a PhD in French studies and has translated more than eighty books, including works by Marguerite Duras, Jean Echenoz, Emmanuel Carrère, Patrick Chamoiseau, Marie Darrieussecq, and Roland Barthes. A Chevalier de l'Ordre des Arts et des Lettres, she has won the 2004 International Dublin Literary Award, the 2006 Scott Moncrieff Prize, and the French-American Foundation Translation Prize (in 1997 and 2008). She lives in Brooklyn.

Jenni Fagan is an award-winning poet, novelist, and screenwriter who has written for the *New York Times*, the *Independent*, and *Marie Claire*. She was named a Scottish Author of the Year by the *Sunday Herald* and one of *Granta*'s Best of Young British Novelists, and has been short-listed for the International Impac Dublin Literary Award, the *Sunday Times* Short Story Award, and the BBC Short

Story Award. She has completed the screenplay of her debut novel, *The Panopticon*, for Sixteen Films. Her directorial debut includes a short film made on the location that inspired the poem "Bangour Village Hospital (or) Edinburgh District Asylum." Fagan's work has been translated into eight languages.

Aminatta Forna is the Windham-Campbell Prize-winning author of the memoir *The Devil That Danced on the Water*, which was shortlisted for the 2003 Samuel Johnson Prize. Her novels include *Ancestor Stones*; *The Memory of Love*, winner of the 2011 Commonwealth Writers' Prize for Best Book; *The Hired Man*, which was chosen as one of the best books of 2013 by National Public Radio and the *Boston Globe*; and *Happiness*. Forna's books have been translated into sixteen languages. She is currently the Lannan Visiting Chair of Poetics at Georgetown University.

Nimmi Gowrinathan is a professor and the founder of the Politics of Sexual Violence Initiative at the City College of New York. Her research and writing examine the impact of sexual violence on women's politics, particularly among female fighters; and through the Beyond Identity fellowship program in Harlem, she works closely with young women of color to help them establish their own political projects.

Aleksandar Hemon is the author of *The Question of Bruno*, *Nowhere Man*, and *The Lazarus Project*. He was awarded a Guggenheim Fellowship in 2003 and a MacArthur Fellowship in 2004. His latest short-story collection, *Love and Obstacles*, was published in 2009, and his collection of autobiographical essays, *The Book of My Lives*, in 2013. He served as editor for the Best European Fiction anthologies, published by Dalkey Archive Press, from 2010 to 2013. His latest novel, *The Making of Zombie Wars*, was published in 2015.

Patrick Hilsman is a New York–based journalist and analyst with experience covering the Middle East and North Africa region with a focus on the Syrian conflict, international weapons traffic, and refugee rights. He was one of the only American journalists who visited East Aleppo between the expulsion of ISIS in early 2014 and the fall of the city to regime forces in late 2016. Hilsman has appeared on BBC World and MSNBC, among other media outlets, and has written for a variety of publications including *Middle East Eye*, *VICE*, the *Daily Beast*, the *Seattle Globalist*, and the *Christian Science Monitor*. His reporting on drone proliferation in the Syrian conflict has been cited by experts at the Center for the Study of the Drone at Bard College.

Nicole Im is a writer based in New York City. She was born and raised in California and recently completed an MFA in nonfiction at the New School.

Etgar Keret is an Israeli writer known for his short stories, graphic novels, and scriptwriting for film and television. His writings have been published in the *New York Times*, the *New Yorker*, *Zoetrope*, and the *Paris Review*, his books in more than forty languages. His latest book, *The Seven Good Years*, was chosen by the *Guardian* as one of the best biographies and memoirs of 2015. Etgar Keret is the winner of the 2016 Charles Bronfman Prize.

Eka Kurniawan was born in Tasikmalaya, Indonesia, in 1975. He studied philosophy at Gadjah Mada University, Yogyakarta, and is the author of novels, short stories, essays, movie scripts, and graphic novels. His novel *Man Tiger* was long-listed for the Man Booker International Prize 2016, and his work has been translated into thirty-four languages. His epic novel of magical realism, *Beauty Is a Wound*, described as a "howling masterpiece" by Chigozie Obioma in the *Millions*, has been widely praised internationally. The *New York Review of Books* considers Kurniawan "a literary child of Günter Grass, Gabriel García Márquez, and Salman Rushdie," and *Le Monde* has suggested that in the future, Nobel jurors may award him the prize "that Indonesia has never received."

Deborah Landau is the author of three collections of poetry, most recently *The Uses of the Body*. She directs the Creative Writing Program at New York University. Her fourth book, *Soft Targets*, is forthcoming from Copper Canyon Press in 2019.

Barry Lopez, a winner of the National Book Award, is the author of *Arctic Dreams* as well as nine works of fiction and six other works of nonfiction. His stories and essays appear regularly in *Harper's*, *Orion*, and the *Georgia Review*, and in several overseas publications, including *Granta*. He is the recipient of numerous cultural and literary awards and of fellowships from the Guggenheim, Lannan, and National Science Foundations. He lives in western Oregon.

Born in the north of France in the 1990s, **Édouard Louis** has published two novels, *The End of Eddy* and *History of Violence*, both bestsellers translated into more than twenty languages. He is also the editor of a scholarly work on the sociologist Pierre Bourdieu. Compared to Jean Genet's by the *Paris Review*, his books deal with sexuality, violence, and class. He is the coauthor, with the philosopher Geoffroy de Lagasnerie, of "Manifesto for an Intellectual and Political Counteroffensive," published in English by the *Los Angeles Review of Books*.

David Mitchell is the award-winning and bestselling author of *The Bone Clocks*, *The Thousand Autumns of Jacob de Zoet*, *Black Swan Green*, *Cloud Atlas*, *Number9Dream*, and *Ghostwritten*. Twice shortlisted for the Man Booker Prize, Mitchell was named one of the hundred most influential people in the world by *Time* magazine in 2007. With his wife, KA Yoshida, Mitchell co-translated the international bestselling memoir The *Reason I Jump* from the Japanese. His latest novel, *Slade House*, was published in October 2015. He lives in Ireland with his wife and two children.

Kanako Nishi was born in Tehran in 1977, and grew up in Cairo and Osaka. She made her debut as a writer in 2004 with *Aoi* (Blue). In 2007, her novel *Tsutenkaku* (Tower to heaven) won the Sakunosuke Oda Prize. In 2012 she received the first Hayao Kawai Prize for her novel *Fukuwarai* (Funny face). Her masterpiece, *Saraba!* won the prestigious Naoki Prize in 2015. She lives in Tokyo.

Ben Okri has published many books: ten novels, including *The Famished Road*, which won the Booker Prize in 1991, *The Age of Magic*, *Dangerous Love*, *In Arcadia*, and *Astonishing the Gods*; three collections of short stories; three collections of essays; and three volumes of poems, the latest being *Wild*. His work has been translated into twenty-six languages. He has been a Fellow Commoner in Creative Arts at Trinity College, Cambridge, and is a Fellow of the Royal Society of Literature. He was awarded an OBE. His books have won numerous international prizes, including the Commonwealth Writer's Prize for Africa, the *Paris Review*'s Aga Khan Prize for Fiction, the Chianti Ruffino-Antico Fattore International Literary Prize, and the Grinzane Cavour Prize. The recipient of many honorary doctorates, he is a vice president of the English Centre of International PEN and was presented with the Crystal Award by the World Economic Forum for his outstanding contribution to the arts and cross-cultural understanding. He also wrote the script for the film *N: The Madness of Reason*. An honorary fellow of Mansfield College, Oxford, he was born in

Nigeria and lives in London. His latest book is *The Magic Lamp: Dreams of Our Age*.

Allison Markin Powell is a literary translator, editor, and publishing consultant in New York City. Her translation of Hiromi Kawakami's *Strange Weather in Tokyo* (originally published as *The Briefcase*) was nominated for the Man Asian Literary Prize and the Independent Foreign Fiction Prize. Her other translations include works by Osamu Dazai, Fuminori Nakamura, and Kaho Nakayama. She maintains the database Japanese Literature in English.

Josephine Rowe is an Australian writer of fiction, poetry, and essays. She is the author of two short-story collections and a novel, *A Loving, Faithful Animal*, published in the United States by Catapult (2017). Rowe holds fellowships from the International Writing Program at the University of Iowa and the Wallace Stegner Program at Stanford University. She currently lives in Tasmania.

Chris Russell is a visual artist whose art and writing have been published in *The Believer*, *Literary Hub*, *Muftah*, *Poetry Ireland Review*, and *Higher Arc*, among other places. He is the associate art editor and a contributing illustrator for *Stonecutter: A Journal of Art and Literature* and is currently working on a graphic translation of Witold Gombrowicz's *Cosmos*, forthcoming from Siglio Press. He lives in Queens, New York, and works in the field of deaf-blindness and special education.

Elif Shafak is the acclaimed author of fifteen books, ten of which are novels, including *The Bastard of Istanbul* and *The Forty Rules of Love*, and is the most widely read female writer in Turkey. Her work has been translated into more than forty languages and she contributes to publications worldwide, including the *New York Times*, *Financial Times*, the *Guardian*, *Der Spiegel*, and *La Repubblica*. As an advocate for women's and LGBT rights and freedom of speech, she is also a public speaker and a TED Global speaker. Shafak has been awarded the Chevalier de l'Ordre des Arts et des Lettres. Her latest novel is *Three Daughters of Eve*.

Sondra Silverston is a native New Yorker who has lived in Israel since 1970. Among her published translations are works by Israeli authors Amos Oz, Etgar Keret, Eshkol Nevo, Savyon Liebrecht, and Aharon Megged. Her translation of Amos Oz's *Between Friends* won the National Jewish Book Award for fiction in 2013.

Leïla Slimani is the first Moroccan woman to win France's most prestigious literary prize, the Prix Goncourt, which she was awarded for her novel *Chanson douce* (*The Perfect Nanny*). A journalist and frequent commentator on women's and human rights, she is French president Emmanuel Macron's personal representative for the promotion of French language and culture. Born in Rabat, Morocco, in 1981, she now lives in Paris with her French husband and their two young children.

Tracy K. Smith is the author of four volumes of poetry, including, most recently, *Wade in the Water*, and *Life on Mars*, which won the Pulitzer Prize. Her memoir, *Ordinary Light*, was a finalist for the National Book Award in nonfiction.

Annie Tucker translates Indonesian literature. She was the recipient of a PEN/Heim Translation Fund award for her translation of Eka Kurniawan's *Beauty Is a Wound*, which was a New York Times Notable book of 2015 and won the World Reader's Award in 2016.

A Yi is a Chinese writer living in Beijing. He worked as a police officer before becoming editor in chief of the literary magazine *Chutzpah*. He is the author of two collections of short stories and has published fiction in *Granta* and the *Guardian*. His first novel, *A Perfect Crime*, has been translated into English, Spanish, French, and German, among other languages, and his second novel will be published in English in 2018.

About the Editor

John Freeman was the editor of *Granta* until 2013. His books include *How to Read a Novelist*, *Tales of Two Cities*, and *Tales of Two Americas*. *Maps*, his debut collection of poems, was published by Copper Canyon in 2017. He is the executive editor at *Literary Hub* and teaches at the New School and New York University. His work has appeared in the *New Yorker* and the *Paris Review* and has been translated into twenty languages.